REVOLUTION

OF

FORMS

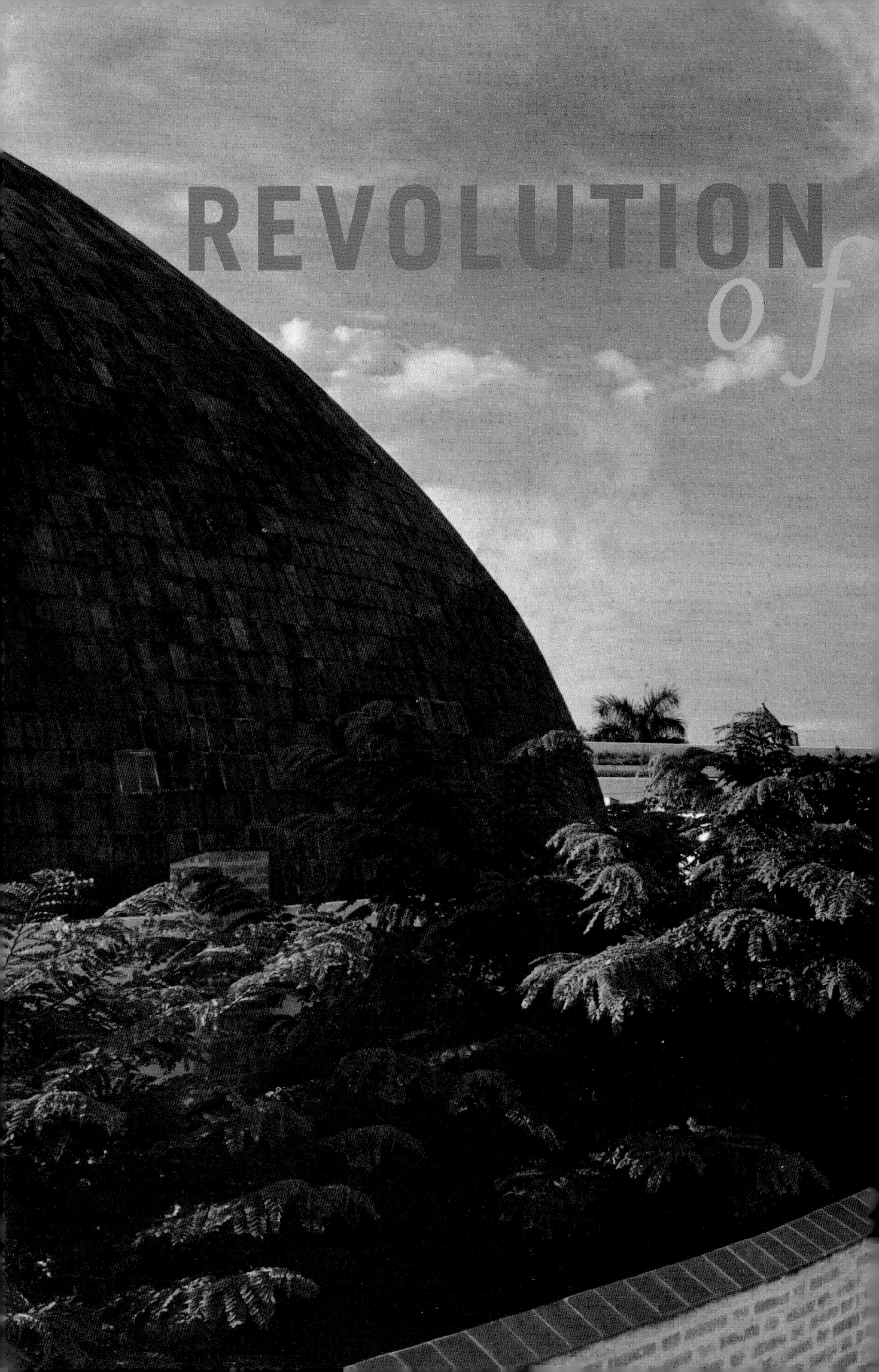
REVOLUTION
of

fo r m s
CUBA'S FORGOTTEN ART SCHOOLS
UPDATED EDITION

JOHN A. LOOMIS

FOREWORD BY
GERARDO MOSQUERA

PRINCETON ARCHITECTURAL PRESS / NEW YORK

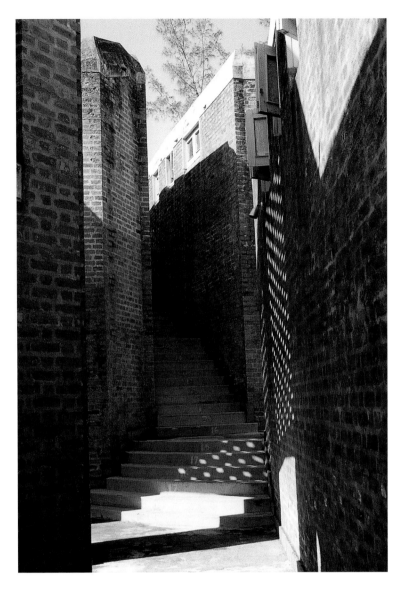

SUPPORT FOR THIS PROJECT
HAS BEEN GENEROUSLY PROVIDED BY

The Getty Research Institute
for the History of Art and the Humanities

The Graham Foundation
for Advanced Studies in the Fine Arts

The Reed Foundation

PUBLISHED BY
Princeton Architectural Press
37 East 7th Street
New York, NY 10003

For a free catalog of books, call 1.800.722.6657.
Visit our website at www.papress.com.

 First edition 1999
Updated edition 2011
Printed and bound in China
14 13 12 11 4 3 2 1

Front cover: Ricardo Porro, School of Modern Dance. Photograph by John A. Loomis.
Back cover: Fidel Castro and John A. Loomis. Photograph by Steven M. Glazer.

Editor and designer of original edition: Therese Kelly
Editor of the updated edition: Linda Lee
Designer of the updated edition: Bree Anne Apperley
Cover design of the updated edition: Connie Hwang

Special thanks to: Sara Bader, Nicola Bednarek Brower, Janet Behning, Megan Carey, Becca Casbon, Carina Cha, Thomas Cho, Penny (Yuen Pik) Chu, Russell Fernandez, Jan Haux, John Myers, Katharine Myers, Margaret Rogalski, Dan Simon, Andrew Stepanian, Jennifer Thompson, Paul Wagner, Joseph Weston, and Deb Wood of Princeton Architectural Press—Kevin C. Lippert, Publisher

LIBRARY OF CONGRESS CATALOGING-IN-PUBLICATION DATA
Loomis, John A., 1951–
Revolution of forms : Cuba's forgotten art schools / John A. Loomis ; foreword by Gerardo Mosquera. — Updated ed.
p. cm.
Includes bibliographical references.
ISBN 978-1-56898-988-4 (alk. paper)
1. Art schools—Cuba—Havana. 2. School buildings—Cuba—Havana. 3. Organic architecture—Cuba—Havana. 4. Communism and architecture—Cuba—Havana. 5. Architecture—Political aspects—Cuba—Havana. 6. Architecture—Cuba—History—20th century. 7. Cubanacán (Havana, Cuba)—Buildings, structures, etc. 8. Porro, Ricardo, 1925– 9. Garatti, Vittorio, 1927– 10. Gottardi, Roberto, 1927– I. Title. II. Title: Cuba's forgotten art schools.
NA6602.A76L66 2011
727'.4709729124—dc22

2010033236

Fidel Castro and Che Guevara playing golf. (ALBERTO KORDA)

Dedicated to the memories of
J. Max Bond Jr.
and
Hugo Consuegra Sosa.

And to my mother and father,
Sue and John Loomis,
and my son,
LaDuke Ely Loomis.

For me this site of creativity, this space of radical open-ness and cultural practice is a margin—a profound edge. Locating oneself there is difficult yet necessary. It is not a "safe" place. One is always at risk....[M]arginality nourishes one's capacity to resist. It offers the possibility of radical perspectives from which to see and create, to imagine alternatives, new worlds.

—bell hooks

TABLE OF CONTENTS

Acknowledgments

My first introduction to the Escuelas Nacionales de Arte (National Art
Schools) came from a lecture by J. Max Bond, Jr. in which he presented
Ricardo Porro's School of Plastic Arts, spoke about its African references and
how it in turn had influenced his own Dr. Martin Luther King Center for
Social Change in Atlanta (Bond, Ryder, James Architects, 1981). Shortly
after, I had an opportunity to visit Cuba in January of 1981 on an architectural tour organized through the Planning Department of Columbia University.
However, the National Art Schools in Cubanacán were not on the itinerary
prepared by our Cuban hosts. "It is too far away," we were told. "The bus
does not have enough gas." "Our presence might interrupt classes in ses-
sion." Finally, after much insistence, we were driven up to the entrance of the
School of Plastic Arts, given a five-minute photo opportunity, a brief explanation of why it was inappropriate architecture for the Cuban Revolution (the
skylights leaked, etc.) and quickly whisked away, many of us not even realizing that we had seen only one fifth of the complex.

I returned to Cuba in 1991 for the VIth Bienal in Havana. There I had the
opportunity to meet architect Roberto Gottardi, who along with architects
Ricardo Porro and Vittorio Garatti, had designed the National Art Schools.
Dismayed at my ignorance about the schools, he proposed to guide me
through the complex. The next afternoon, we spent several hours walking
through an almost magic realist, and at times Piranesian, architecture and
landscape. During our explorations, he recounted his story of the project. I
found it most compelling that such a unique architectural masterpiece could
fall from grace. That afternoon was the beginning of what became by and
large an oral history project that has taken six years to document, leading me
to long conversations with not only Roberto Gottardi in Havana, but also
Ricardo Porro in Paris and Vittorio Garatti in Milan, as well as others, both
Cuban and non-Cuban, who had been involved in the project. But it is these
three architects to whom I am most deeply indebted. They all gave generously
of their time, their personal archives, and their patience in acquainting me
with the nuances and complexities of those early years of the Cuban Revolution and with the creativity and the hopes it generated. And I am also grateful
to Elena Porro, Wanda Garatti, and Luz Maria Gottardi, who contributed their
homes, their hospitality, and their own memories.

The Getty Research Institute, thanks to its former director, Kurt Forster, and
its former deputy director, Thomas Ford Reese, provided me the opportunity
to do research and to present the first public lecture on the National Art
Schools while I was in residence as a visiting scholar in 1994. The Graham
Foundation for the Arts provided financial support for research that was
essential to the completion of this project. To them and their director,

Richard Solomon, I owe special gratitude. The Reed Foundation provided assistance that enabled us to enhance the quality of this book's production. Jane Gregory Rubin, the director of Interamericas, a program of the New York Foundation for the Arts, provided thoughtful comments that further enlightened me as to the importance of Afro-Cuban culture.

I am very grateful to many colleagues in Cuba who provided both material assistance and contributed to my understanding of the context in which the story of the schools developed. Sergio Baroni, Tania Bruguera, Mario Coyula Cowley, Emilio Escobar Loret de Mola, Roberto Fernándo Rizzo, José Alberto Figueroa, Ever Fonseca, Víctor Marín, Rosendo Mesías, José Mosquera, Eduardo Luis Rodríguez, María Cristina Vives Gutiérrez, and José Gregorio Veigas Zamora were all generous with their information, insight, and criticism. Roberto Segre and the late Fernando Salinas, early critics of the schools who later adopted more inclusive positions, provided my first introduction to architecture in Cuba, without which the telling of this story would have never occurred. Understandably, not all in Cuba whom I approached were willing to speak. One important cultural official politely begged off saying that the beauty and the sadness of the story of the schools made it too painful to recount.

Then there are those Cubans who are no longer in Cuba. In Paris are David Bigelman and Gilberto Seguí Diviñó, both of whom worked on the schools as young architects. The late Manuel Granados, a Cuban writer also in Paris, provided insights into the complexitites of Afro-Cuban culture and its relation to contemporary politics. In Los Angeles my gratitude extends to Silverio Bosch, Ignacio Fernández, Rosa Lowinger, Adolfo Nodal and Rafael Oceguera. In Miami I am grateful to Humberto Alonso, José Gelabert-Navia, Raúl Rodríguez and especially to Nicolás Quintana who was helpful in providing background information on the 1950s. Max Borges, Jr. in Virginia kindly provided photographs from his archives. In New York, I am thankful for the comments of Roberto de Alba and especially Hugo Consuegra, who was one of the last critics to courageously and publicly defend the schools in Cuba in 1965, and who generously made available to me his personal archives and unpubished memoirs.

Critical early opportunities to travel to Cuba were provided by my former Dean, J. Max Bond, Jr., and Associate Dean Alan Feigenberg at the School of Architecture and Environmental Studies of the City College of New York. The school's chair, Donald Ryder, and other colleagues generously indulged in my absence from teaching responsibilities while preparing the manuscript. Gratitude also goes to Lorne Buchman, President; Stephen Beal, Provost; and David Meckel, Dean of Architecture, of the California College of Arts and Crafts, for providing me with new opportunities and horizons.

Paolo Gasparini provided access to his splendid archive of photographs, taken in 1965 shortly after the opening of the schools. José Figueroa and Hazel Hankin shared other striking photographic images. Steve Callis provided other invaluable photographic services. Alex Brito, William Duncanson and their computer skills rehabilitated graphic images which had long ago deteriorated in the Ministry of Construction's archives.

Many others have helped in memorable ways. Norma Barbacci, Harriet Bee, Horst Berger, Julia Bloomfield, Jean Carey Bond, Guido Canella, Zeynep Çelik, Marco Cenzati, Tonino Civitelli, Margaret Crawford, Jerrilynn Dodds, John Fernández, Anna Foppiano, Geoffrey Fox, Kenneth Frampton, Graziano Gasparini, Angela Giral, Hansel Hernández, Narciso Menocal, John de Monchaux, Maria Oliver, Elizabeth Padjen, Janet Parks, Carol McMichael Reese, Arthur and Cynthia Rosenzweig, Peter Rowe, Jorge Silvetti, Nancy Stout, Susana Torre, Paul Turner, Lauretta Vinciarelli, Ricardo Zurita and the Center for Cuban Studies, all deserve thanks for information, support and/or kindnesses large and small.

For recognizing the value in publishing these masterful works which are virtually unpublished and unknown, I am certainly grateful to Princeton Architectural Press, Kevin C. Lippert, Clare Jacobson and especially my editor Therese Kelly for daring to go forth where others feared to tread.

This exercise in micro-history also seeks to shed light on the larger historical context and vice versa. In addition to the formal sources cited in the bibliography and notes, my research has relied also upon informal sources or what is now being referred to by scholars as "unofficial knowledge." Oral accounts make up an important part of this research as well as a uniquely Cuban institution, *la bola*, or as we would say, "the grapevine." In Cuba this is sometimes the only source of information, especially if the news might be embarrassing to the government. Inevitably, such informal sources carry a certain amount of subjectivity, and accounts do not always agree. But this is also true of formal sources. Finally I wish to thank all those who took the time to read my manuscript, offering their comments and criticism: Ricardo Porro, Roberto Gottardi, Vittorio Garatti, Greg Castillo, Margaret Crawford, Eduardo Luis Rodríguez, Richard Ingersoll, and Roberto Segre. Here too, not all necessarily shared the same recollections or points of view. Nevertheless, I have striven to be scrupulous as to accuracy and objectivity, but take full responsibility for any errors in fact or interpretation that may have occurred.

Closing gratitude goes to my father and mother, John and Sue Loomis, and to my wife, Dee LaDuke and son, LaDuke Ely Loomis.

FOREWORD

by Gerardo Mosquera

This book uncovers one of the most strange and fascinating stories of all of modern architecture. A story of a group of buildings absolutely exceptional for their originality, for the extraordinary circumstances of their origin—to which they continue to be obsessively chained today—and for the polemics which free them. It is also a story of a complicated short-circuit between aesthetics, ideology, culture, and politics. In this way, the volume serves as an architectural analysis of the works and at the same time dissects the ideological-cultural confrontations in the midst of which they were built, and from which the passage of time has not been able to liberate them. It is the first book dedicated to the Schools of Art of Havana, today almost in ruins, and I cannot help feeling a certain archeological nostalgia, as with such books that bring to light the secrets of a "lost city." Here, architecture plays the leading role in a captivating story, one that *Revolution of Forms* tells for the first time in such depth that, without diminishing its scholarly rigor, I would venture to say that we are at the beginning of an "architectural novel."

The book narrates how the Schools of Art were born of the initial utopia of the Cuban Revolution—which, maintaining a certain independence from the tenets of the Soviet block, contributed a good deal to the development of the general ideals of liberation in the 1960s—how they fell in disgrace and remain in oblivion. In the same way that people, books, paintings, and films are marginalized in totalitarian regimes, these buildings were also purged. Beyond any publicity received initially, this situation made their international diffusion difficult. With the advent of postmodern architecture at the start of the 1980s, Ricardo Porro's School of Plastic Arts was cited as a pioneer example of a kind of exotic pre-post-modern work.[1] John A. Loomis considers the Schools instead under the most precise label of "other" modernism, relating them to the postulates

---

1. Paolo Portoghesi, *Postmodern* (Rizzoli, 1983). An excerpt from *Postmodern* appears in the Documents section at the end of this book.

of Ernesto Rogers, among others. Nevertheless, if we accept the existence of a postmodern conciousness, overall as a critical rupture from modern monisms, there is no doubt that the Schools are an example of how the notion of postmodernity can be consequence and not description "of a realigned universe" by the practice of societies previously displaced completely, as Geeta Kapur affirms.[2]

Until now, the Schools have been insufficiently analyzed due to lack of information. It is enough to review the bibliography at the end of this book to perceive the lack of international references. They have remained more as documental reference, in the manner of the first sketches of the Mayan ruins. Some architects and critics who visited Cuba were guided privately by friends—almost always without the official permission necessary to see the buildings, and were impressed by what they saw. Their impressions arose from an architecture as singular and attractive as unknown, reinforced by the lamentable state of the buildings, which in the extreme case of the School of Ballet, is a ruin abandoned in the middle of the jungle, a Tikal of the 1960s. The Schools of Art are the first postmodern ruins. Yet they arrived at this state by the crisis of a modern project, united in their contradictions with it. This situation is even more unusual because they are living ruins—with the exception of the School of Ballet—inhabited, just like their own city of Havana. The buildings have served also as the seat of the Instituto Superior de Arte, "*foyer*" to the transcendental movement of cultural renovation which took place in the decade of the 1980s. This book finally puts on the map these singular works, a study of their defining features.

But the importance of *Revolution of Forms* goes beyond the architectonic; it is one of the few analyses that I know of which treats the cultural context of the Cuban Revolution during its first decade of existence. This analysis is of great importance because this decade was the period in which Cuba, in all of its history, had the most influence on the rest of the world. Not only for having brought us to the edge of nuclear disaster and having fomented guerilla movements in the Third World, but also for its place in the ideological-cultural configuration that we call in the West "the '60s." Today the Cuban '60s have been somewhat mythologized—even I have contributed to this—as an epoch of extraordinary enthusiasm and cultural blossoming, supported by more liberal politics. This characteristic stands out overall in comparison to the following decade, when Cuba fully entered the Soviet orbit. If the aforementioned is true, as it has been presented here, this book also has the virtue of indirectly deconstructing the myth of the '60s by presenting us with a much more problematic image. The case of the Schools of Art is a good example of the ideological extremism and repressive authoritarianism that accompanied the Cuban socialist

---

2. Geeta Kapur, "Contemporary Cultural Practice: Some Polemical Categories," *Third Text* 11 (London, Summer 1990): 116.

process from its origins, even when during "the hard years" it would become less clear due to the rigors of the revolutionary struggles and the utopian ingenuousness of the time. Even more so, the Schools are a sort of fossil of ideoesthetic debate corresponding to another epoch. The persistence of the practice of the ideological clichés with repsect to these works, more than amazing us by their absurdity, alert us to the conservatism of power.

This book is also quite interesting for its discussion of context in architecture. This is an important point, as the architects Vittorio Garatti, Roberto Gottardi, and especially Ricardo Porro (an architect-artist reminiscent of Gaudí) all worked with a clear will to symbolize, in a manner similar to the work of the plastic artist. In this way, the School of Plastic Arts is practically an inhabitable sculpture, more for its symbolic discourse than for its formal emphasis. In spite of this aspect, the debate around the Schools makes clear the political virulence that the ideological and cultural signifiers of architecture can unleash. The relationship between revolution and modernism is evident. If during the October Revolution in Russia the architects defined modernism as the universal medium for the social utopia and revolutionary culture, the Schools define the initial moment of the Cuban Revolution as an answer to international modernism from the periphery, both symbolically and ethnoculturally. This emphasizes their ties with nationalism, the Third World, and Cuban socialism, and their conflicts with pseudorational and pseudopragmatic modernization.

In reviewing the course of vicissitudes that Loomis recounts to us in his book, a question emerges. What does the future hold for the Schools of Art? A famous Latin American novel, José Eustasio Rivera's *La Vorágine*, ends with a frightening sentence which acquires metaphoric connotations for so many histories of our continent. "*Los devoró la selva.*" (The jungle devoured them.) Hopefully, the decisive contribution of *Revolution of Forms* to validate these extraordinary architectural masterpieces will bring about concrete steps to save them, and they will continue to perform the functions for which they were created.

Gerardo Mosquera
Havana, 1998

History, to paraphrase Fidel Castro, has absolved the Escuelas Nacionales de Arte (National Art Schools). An unintended consequence of the first edition of *Revolution of Forms: Cuba's Forgotten Art Schools* was the preservation and restoration of the schools. History books are typically passive documents, but it appears that *Revolution of Forms* acted as an active agent of change.

Chapter Six, "Road to Rehabilitation," maps out the political and cultural changes that took place from the early 1980s to 1998 in Cuba that contributed to a reappraisal of the schools. These shifts included the activities of a group of brilliant and brave young artists known as the Generation of the Eighties, who gave new critical expression to art in Cuba and provided an intellectual framework for reexamining the schools in the context of the Revolution. Fortunately, these young critics were supported by sympathetic government officials, who understood the importance of the freedom of artistic expression. This new openness began to influence the practice of architecture in Cuba. It also provoked the rethinking of the schools and the "rehabilitation" of the architects. Outside Cuba, the New York City–based World Monuments Fund placed the schools on their Watch List and advocated steadfastly for their recognition and preservation. Although these acts were in play as the book went to press, the actual publication of *Revolution of Forms* was a critical accelerator that had a catalytic effect on the events to come.

During the final year in which the book was being prepared, Havana's notorious rumor mill (*la bola*) kicked into gear. A government official addressed a gathering of the Union of Architects and Engineers: "There is an architect in the United States, an enemy of Cuba, being paid by the CIA, to write a book about the National Art Schools in order to make Cuba and the Revolution look bad. And we have to do something about this."[1] Ironically, he later became involved in restoring the schools, and when we met a few years later, he greeted me with great enthusiasm,

1. This information was received by word of mouth in Spanish by the author from a colleague who attended the meeting and wishes to not be identified.

asked me to sign his copy of the book, and only left after giving me a big *abrazo* (hug).

Revolution of Forms was launched in March 1999 at two high-profile events that drew considerable attention. In Los Angeles, the launch took place at R. M. Schindler's Kings Road House at the MAK Center, with an exhibition of photos of the schools by Paolo Gasparini taken in 1965. Conceived by Peter Noever, CEO and artistic director of the MAK Vienna, curated by Carol McMichael Reese, the director of MAK Center Los Angeles, and sponsored by the Austrian Ministry of Culture, the event reunited Ricardo Porro, Vittorio Garatti, and Roberto Gottardi for an emotional first time since 1966, when they had last seen each other in Havana. Thom Mayne, Eric Owen Moss, Mark Mack, and other local "architecturati" in attendance lavished well-deserved praise on the three septuagenarian architects, who were not used to such attention.

The exhibition and opening event were replicated later the same week at Columbia University in New York, with support from the Cooper-Hewitt Museum. There, Bernard Tschumi, Kenneth Frampton, and others paid their enthusiastic respects to the three architects. Also present were expatriate former students and colleagues. This included artist, architect, and former government official Hugo Consuegra Sosa, who had distinguished himself from other supporters, who were by now afraid, by launching a lone last-ditch public defense of the schools in 1965. In most cases, these Cubans had not seen the three architects for more than thirty years. It was a heartfelt reunion. The exhibit later traveled to Austria, then elsewhere in Europe and the United States. Needless to say, these events generated copious press, including two articles in the *New York Times*, which were closely followed by government officials in Cuba.

Meanwhile, unknown to those outside of Cuba, things were taking place inside the country. And in late October 1999, I received an unexpected phone call from Paris from Ricardo Porro, shortly followed by another call from Milan from Vittorio Garatti. They sounded like excited school boys, and both said—somewhat breathlessly—that they had just received a phone call from a vice minister from the Ministry of Finance in Cuba inviting them to a meeting in December to discuss the future plans and budget for the preservation and restoration of the National Art Schools. They both attributed this unanticipated proposition to the groundswell of interest generated by *Revolution of Forms*.

It so happened that la bola had been particularly active among architects and other cultural figures in Cuba since the March publication of *Revolution of Forms*. On October 6, 1999, at the annual meeting of the national congress of the Union of Cuban Writers and Artists (UNEAC) with the Council of State, there was a discussion about the cultural role of architecture in Cuba. For the first time ever in this venue, architecture was considered as a cultural construct, not one that was merely functional and social. When architects were first allowed to join UNEAC in the mid-1980s, the organization began to reevaluate the importance of Cuba's five-hundred-year legacy of architectural treasures. The former discomfort felt by the revolutionaries with the architecture of their colonial and capitalist pasts was increasingly giving way to cultural pride as the decade wore on. It reached national proportions at this meeting attended by some of the most powerful Cuban dignitaries, including Castro himself. Mario Coyula, an architect and an important cultural figure, presented an overview of Cuba's vast architectural history. In response, Castro asked about the architecture of the Revolution and its great monuments. José Antonio Choy, an important architect, stood up and replied that, in the context of Cuba's architectural history, they were few. He pointed out that the National Art Schools stand out as magnificent examples of which Cuba should be proud. However, over the years they had been treated very badly. Fidel wanted to know more. The ensuing discussion acknowledged the influence of *Revolution of Forms*—the international attention it had garnered and the many foreign travelers it had attracted to visit the National Art Schools. Unfortunately, the schools were in a far-from-presentable state. Castro closed the meeting with this declaration:

> The schools exist, and they have a history, a most beautiful history. Perhaps one of the most beautiful histories. In the middle of so many obstacles and difficulties...they killed a beloved young girl—like a first love. This is how I felt the day when they told me of the sentence of death for the project. We need to propose to finish the schools—but completely! Like that beloved young girl, the school with which I had fallen in love, that day when I entered the complex, ignorant, nevertheless it appeared to me so marvelous, and I liked it so much [applause]...This is what for me is most important: that this work is built as I still remember it. Because I, who know[s] nothing of architecture, only remember how very much I liked this project. And I believe that this is an outstanding project.[2]

Shortly thereafter, Castro declared that the schools would be recognized, restored, and preserved as national monuments. (It turns out that Castro had a copy of *Revolution of Forms*.) Things had come full circle from 1961, when Castro had first praised the schools as "the most beautiful academy of art in the world."

John A. Loomis
San Francisco, CA, 2010

2. Videotape transcripts, translated by the author, from the Congreso de la UNEAC (Encuentro con el Consejo Nacional del Estado), Havana, Cuba, October 6, 1999.

ACKNOWLEDGMENTS
TO THE UPDATED EDITION

In addition to the friends and supporters acknowledged in the first edition, I wish to thank Felipe Dulzaides, Alysa Nahmias, and Charles Koppelman. All three have brought their own insightful perspectives to this history, and I have learned much from them all.

Thanks to graphic designer Connie Hwang of Connie Hwang Design who created the *Revolution of Forms* website.

Thanks to Jennifer Thompson, editorial director at Princeton Architectural Press (PAP) and Clare Jacobson, formerly of PAP, for launching this second printing. Linda Lee, the editor of this edition, could not have been a better partner with whom to work. Most significantly, thanks to Kevin Lippert, founder and publisher of PAP. Without his vision and steadfast support, the fate of the National Art Schools may have been very different.

INTRODUCTION

A revolution of forms is

a revolution of essentials.

José Martí

Nearly forty years since the advent of the Cuban Revolution, one complex of buildings stands out as its most compelling work of architecture—the Escuelas Nacionales de Arte (National Art Schools). Constructed in a comandeered country club between 1961 and 1965 and then partially abandoned, they occupy an ambiguous and, even today, controversial place in the architectural canon of the Cuban Revolution. The complex is virtually unknown among works of contemporary architecture, its story buried in history just as some of its buildings lie buried in the verdant landscape. Created by one Cuban architect, Ricardo Porro, and two Italians, Roberto Gottardi and Vittorio Garatti, the schools express the revolutionary passion and utopian optimism of a unique moment when the Cuban Revolution appeared, as Ricardo Porro has described it, "*más surrealista que socialista.*"

Despite their various states of deterioration today, the evocative and poetic qualities of the schools are nevertheless still apparent in their expressive forms. Moreover, the story behind the schools provides insights into the relationships among politics, culture and power in a small, insular Marxist-Leninist state struggling to reconcile conflicting realities. Cuba may appear from the outside to be a monolithic Marxist-Leninist construct, but in reality it is a permeable assemblage of competing and often conflicting political, economic and—class—interests that present a range of complexities and contradictions. The architects of the National Art Schools came out on the losing end of a drama framed by those particular contradictions of the early years of the Cuban Revolution. The values that they chose to represent Cuban socialism proved not to be in accordance with those later promoted by the Soviet Union. Nevertheless, through their expressive independence, Porro, Gottardi and Garatti created the works of architecture that most successfully embody the hopes and aspirations of the young Cuban Revolution.

In addition to representing a unique revolutionary political and cultural environment, the National Art Schools also very much engaged in the contradictions that formed the architectural debates of the early 1960s internationally: expressionism vs. rationalism, appropriate technologies vs. advanced technologies, and cultural identity vs. universal values. In each of these polemics, the architects took the less favored position, oppositional to the modernist values that had dominated much of architecture into the early 1960s. Polemical stances do not necessarily secure a positive place in history, and this book seeks to rectify this situation.

With few exceptions, existing documentation of the National Art Schools is schematic in nature and of limited accessibility, often in obscure publications. Some of it is highly partisan, and much of it reviews only the work of Ricardo Porro. Critiques often reflect the tendency of European and North American architectural historians to take interest in the architecture of the so-called Third World only when it serves to validate a First-World context. For those seeking to understand the architectural merits of the schools, and moreover, wish to know their history, none of the existing publications are fully satisfactory in presenting Cuba's National Art Schools either as works of architecture or as subjects of an ideological debate. In part the lack of a full accounting of the story of the schools is due to their ambiguous position within Cuba. But in part it is also due to the increasingly incomprehensible economic blockade imposed by the United States that inhibits Cuba's accessibility to researchers and a free intellectual exchange.

Nearly a full decade since the end of the cold war, the National Art Schools still lie somewhere outside Cuba's vision of its own national heritage. This situation, however, is not permanent. Geopolitical changes, as well as changes within Cuba itself, now provide for Cubans an opportunity for a fresh perspective in evaluating the significance of the National Art Schools. Hopefully, they will soon assume a place in both Cuba's architectural history as well as the greater history of contemporary architecture, as critical works that sought to articulate alternative values to mainstream socialism and to mainstream modernism.

John A. Loomis
West Hollywood, CA, 1998

Los caminos de mi Cuba

Nunca van a donde deben.

Carlos Puebla

O N E

In the Beginning

Forging a National Identity

When the Cuban Revolution ushered in the New Year of 1959, both the context and future of Cuban culture were to change profoundly. Creating a revolutionary Cuban identity in all areas of culture became one of the major goals for the Revolution. Internationalist and socialist values were an important part of the developing discourse seeking to define Cuba's new cultural identity.

This discourse had its origins in another revolutionary period. During the late nineteenth century, the cultural debate concerning the nature of Cuban identity—*cubanidad*—had political resonance with the movement for independence from Spain. José Martí, the most important intellectual figure in the struggle for independence, understood that establishing a clear sense of national identity was an essential ideological component to creating a unified patriotic movement to liberate the island from Spanish domination. The idea of the regional specificity of Cuban culture, that is its otherness to Spanish culture, found some of its most coherent expression in Martí's writings, though other intellectuals, such as Félix Varela, had been examining this in the earlier part of the century. One of the important aspects of Martí's writings was his progressive view of race which recognized African as well as Spanish contributions to a common Cuban culture. It is important to note that the leader in the struggle for independence, second only to Martí in importance, was the black general Antonio Maceo and that the majority of the troops under his command were themselves Cubans of African descent. Because of their participation, the wars of independence of 1868 and 1895 were not only struggles for political liberation, but also processes of national and cultural integration.

After independence, *cubanidad* was still in process of definition and continued to be a subject of debate. After the Little War of 1912 and the defeat of Afro-Cuban insurgents who had rebelled against their disenfranchisement by the new independent government, the discussion of race was suppressed for a time in favor of a discussion of culture. Nevertheless,

OPPOSITE: *Wifredo Lam,* Visible/Invisible, *1971*
(COLLECTION OF NARCISO MENOCAL)

beginning in the 1930s the issue of race became an unavoidable component of the cultural debate.

One tendency, *negrismo*, associated with other Latin American intellectual movements influenced by the *negritude* movement of the French-speaking Caribbean, granted African culture equal status with Spanish culture in forming a *cubanidad* that was *mulata*, or mixed race. The ethnographer and historian Fernando Ortiz summed up this position with the words, "Without the Negro, Cuba would not be Cuba."[1] Another tendency, more Hispanic or Creole oriented, did recognize African contributions to Cuban culture, but considered them secondary to Spanish influence in the creation of a *cubanidad* that was *criolla*. Intellectuals such as Alberto Arredondo regarded contemporary interest in black culture as a passing European fad, like the Parisian infatuation with jazz and Josephine Baker, that had little to do with the reality of the Caribbean. To some of these intellectuals, "Afro-Cuban" was an irrelevant concept. The memory of the Little War of 1912, as well as of slavery's unavoidable legacy of racism, accounted for a certain amount of negrophobia on the part of some who wanted to believe that slavery had essentially erased African culture. Many of these Creole oriented intellectuals tended to advocate a process of *blanqueamiento* (whitening) toward achieving a unified national identity. However, *acriollamiento* (creolization) was a process that affected not only blacks but also the descendants of Europeans and represented for many a process for the development of a common culture distinct from both those of Europe and Africa.

It would be a mistake to view issues of cultural identity in Cuba simply in bipolar racial terms or framed by North American experience. The Negrista and Creole tendencies did not always function in opposition or in tension. They often coexisted, intimately interconnected. Some intellectuals, such as the writer Alejo Carpentier, published in journals that represented differing cultural positions regarding race and ethnicity. Shared among all Cuban intellectuals was a desire to articulate a distinctly Cuban cultural identity, within a strongly anti-imperialist, nationalist agenda.[2]

Beginning in the late 1920s, literature became an important medium for the exploration of identity and the development of Afro-Cuban and other cultural themes. In 1930 Nicolás Guillen published his first African-inspired work, *Motivos de Son*. Alejo Carpentier's first novel, *¡Ecue-Yamba-O!*, likewise drew from Afro-Cuban religion. Cuban literature of this period also addressed *cubanidad* through the elaboration of other regional and cultural specific themes such as the tropical environment, machismo, the *guajiro*, and sensuality. Such themes found their way into *Origines*, what was considered the most important literary journal in the Spanish-speaking world, edited by José Lezama Lima (1910–1976) and published from 1944 to 1956.

ABOVE: *Amelia Peláez*, Marpacifico, *1936*
(PRIVATE COLLECTION, MIAMI)

ABOVE RIGHT: *René Portocarrero*, Interiores del Cerro, *1943*
(PRIVATE COLLECTION, MIAMI)

Painting was also an important venue for the expression of identity. Cuban art historian Narciso Menocal points out that

> In Europe establishing new definitions of form and pictorial space were major concerns, as is evident in Cubism, German Expressionism or the *neue Sachlichkeit*—however different from each other these movements may have been and whatever their respective iconographical agendas were. In Cuban art, by contrast, establishing a national imagery through a search for the characteristic and exploring national identity were the major issues.[3]

And indeed, *cubanidad* was central to the work of Cuba's artists in the 1930s and 1940s who explored the island's African heritage, Creole culture, and tropical environment. Amelia Peláez (1896–1968) developed a "tropical Cubist" idiom that celebrated decorative and architectural elements from everyday Cuban life. Her abstract forms are both sensuous and organic in character. The work of Luis Martínez Pedro (1920–1989) drew from Afro-Cuban ritual and the indigenous Taino heritage. René Portocarrero's (1912–1985) early work had thematic populist similarities to that of Diego Rivera. His work of the 1940s explored memory and nostalgia through the renderings of colonial interiors in the *Interiores del Cerro* series. The body of work of this period sufficiently impressed Alfred Barr such that he organized an exhibition at the Museum of Modern Art in 1944 entitled *Modern Cuban Painters*. In the catalogue he commented upon the degree of regional and national expression in Cuban art:

Wifredo Lam, La Jungla, *1943*

There is almost no painting of the Cuban scene comparable to our often literal or sentimental painting of the American scene, and there is little obvious regional and nationalistic feeling. Cuban color, Cuban light, Cuban forms and Cuban motifs are plastically and imaginatively assimilated rather than realistically represented.[4]

An artist whose work grew out of this period and went on to transcend it was Wifredo Lam (1902–82). Of mixed Chinese, African, and Spanish heritage, Lam fused the experience of European modernism, especially surrealism, with that of his own cultural, especially African, identity. Not only a cultural radical, Lam was a political radical, a self-declared Marxist long before the Cuban Revolution who remained closely identified with the Revolution until his death, despite long periods of residence abroad. Lam's work, often agressively sensual and sexual, is unique in how it transcends the specifics of iconography to penetrate the essence of Afro-Cuban culture from within. Cuban art critic Gerardo Mosquera describes Lam's work as "the first vision ever of modern art from the standpoint of Africa within Latin America. . . [representing] a synthesis that might be endorsed by modernity, thus creating a non-Western space within the Western tradition, decentralizing it, transforming and de-Europeanizing it."[5]

Despite a conscious presence in art and literature, Afro-Cuban issues tended not to be expressed in the parallel debate that emerged in the late 1930s regarding architectural identity in Cuba. This is partly due to the enormous physical presence of the Spanish colonial legacy and the comparative lack of African spatial legacy in Cuba. This Hispanic architectural legacy was first and most consciously documented by Joaquín E. Weiss y Sánchez (1894–1968) in 1936 in his seminal book, *Arquitectura cubana colonial*.[6] Weiss, an architect and historian, educated at Cornell (1916) and at the University of Havana (1919), was a professor of architectural history until 1962. He was an early proponent of the cultural value of the built colonial heritage and an advocate of historic preservation. Yet, as Jorge Rigau points out,

> Weiss's *La arquitectura colonial cubana*, Cuba's preeminent text on Havana's early architectural efforts, could today be reread as a text on Spanish influences, rather than as a testament to Cuban achievements. Not that it could have been otherwise. In the early decades of the twentieth century, Latin American intellectuals repeatedly validated their built heritage based on comparisons to the Old World, and Weiss, in keeping with the times, assumed filiation to be sufficient clarification. Adjectives like baroque, neochurrigueresque, and Andalusian—in spite of their imprecise, yet frequent application—were imported to dignify Caribbean architecture. But in the end, buildings so labeled had been inaccurately endowed with a distant coat of arms. This "elsewhere-centered" cultural explanation has always stopped short of indigenous validation.[7]

Inside an eighteenth century colonial court- yard in Trinidad with typical medio punto *and louvered openings* (JOHN A. LOOMIS)

The importance of Cuba's *arquitectura criolla* was further validated, and in another "elsewhere-centered" context, in 1947 in the work of Francisco Prat Puig, *El prebarroco en Cuba—una escuela criolla de arquitectura morisca*.[8] Together, Weiss, Prat Puig, and their colleague Pedro Martínez Inclán (1883–1957), another one of Cuba's early preservationists, can be considered important for value they placed on local architectural heritage.

In 1941 the Agrupación Tectónica de Estudios Contemporáneos (ATEC), a group associated with CIAM, was founded to pursue the discussion of contemporary issues of architecture and urbanism within Cuba's environmental and cultural context. Many of the founders of ATEC developed distinguished careers.[9] In 1942–43 ATEC joined with another organization, the Patronato Pro-Urbanismo, headed by Martínez Inclán, to present an exhibition in the center of old Havana, *Trinidad. . . lo que fue, es y será*. The exhibit presented Trinidad, one of Cuba's most beautiful colonial towns, and used this example from history as a platform for debate on issues of contemporary urbanism.

In the conservative atmosphere of the academy, however, there was little attention to issues of *cubanidad* until after World War II. A few Cuban architects, like Weiss, had studied abroad, but most were educated at the architecture school at the Universidad de La Habana, founded in 1900. In 1947, students, lead by Frank Martínez, Ricardo Porro, and Nicolás Quintana, abducted Vignola's books from the library of the architecture school and publicly burned them in the plaza, a symbolic act that declared their allegiance to modernism. This was a youthful act that they have all since disowned with no small amount of embarrassment. Nevertheless, after the "*quema de los Viñola*," the school did depart from its Beaux-Arts origins to embrace a more modernist program, while at the same time seeking to reintegrate values from the island's *arquitectura criolla*. The former students of that era recall it as one particularly charged with debate and energy. There subsequently emerged a sincere desire among mostly younger Cuban architects to create a regionalist architectural language, although within modernist conventions, that would reroute the universalizing tendencies of the International Style.

European and North American exemplars of the International Style

Harrison and Abramovitz, U.S. Embassy, Havana, 1952-53 (J. ALEX LANGLEY)

LEFT TO RIGHT: *Ricardo Porro, Franco Albini, Miguel Gastón, Fernando Salinas, and Enrique Govantes with model of proposed development for Habana del Este*

(COURTESY R. SEGRE)

were no strangers to the island. Walter Gropius, at the invitation of students Frank Martínez, Nicolás Quintana, and Ricardo Porro, lectured in Havana in 1945, as did Richard Neutra. Neutra returned in 1956 to design the Casa Schulthess in the exclusive Country Club Park suburb. Harrison and Abramowitz designed the U.S. Embassy (1952–53). Welton Becket (with Arroyo y Menéndez) designed the Havana Hilton (1958), renamed the Havana Libre after the Revolution. Josep Lluís Sert had visited the island briefly in 1939 on his way to the United States as a refugee from the Spanish civil war. He was retained with Paul Lester Wiener as consultant to the Junta Nacional de Planificación for the development of a new regional plan (1955–58) of epic proportions. It went unrealized, and fortunately so for colonial Havana, which would have lost or had radically altered much of its historic core. Philip Johnson paid a visit in 1955 in anticipation of a hotel and casino project that was not realized.[10] In 1958 Franco Albini came to collaborate with Gastón y Domínguez on urban planning proposals for Habana del Este, newly developing suburbs to the east of the bay. At the time of the Cuban Revolution itself, Mies Van der Rohe had on the boards a project, offices for Bacardí in Santiago de Cuba, that was never realized.

A significant number of Cuban architects participated in the international scene of the time and sent representatives to CIAM meetings six through ten.[11] The regionalist and vernacular interests that were on the margins of CIAM paralleled similar debates in Cuba. These are illustrated in two seminal studies: *Los bateyes de los centrales azucareros* (1951) by Eugenio Batista and Alberto Beale; and *Las villas pesqueras* (1953) by Frank Martínez, Ricardo Porro, René Calvache, Alberto Beale, and Nicolás Quintana. Adding to this lively intellectual environment was an architectural practice formed in 1952 called Arquitectos Unidos and headed by Humberto Alonso (b. 1924). The Colegio Instituto Edison (1953–54) and the offices of the Colegio de Arquitectos (1953–55) are two of their works. But of equal or greater importance to their built work, Arquitectos Unidos served as an intellectual forum, a scene of weekly "tumultuous and uncontrollable *tertulias*," salons, that debated current issues in architecture, arts, and politics.[12]

Allied with Arquitectos Unidos was a group of painters known as Los Once (painter and architect Hugo Consuegra (b. 1929) was a member of both). Los Once rejected the "*tropicalismo*" that characterized the art of the preceding decade in favor of an abstraction that assumed a more international perspective. At the same time, their avant-gardist rebellion was connected to their political opposition of the Batista dictatorship. They openly refused to participate in officially sponsored exhibitions, and organized counter-exhibitions as acts of political defiance. It is interesting to note that while Lam, Peláez, and Portocarrero continued to work in a figurative venue, their work now assumed a more abstract elaboration of their culturally oriented themes during the 1950s.

In this same period, architecture was generally manifesting itself in Cuba in three ways: the monumentalist public works of the Batista dictatorship, the International Style buildings that were proliferating in areas of real-estate speculation like the commercial and residential El Vedado district, and the small experimental projects, mostly houses, that explored regionalism and *cubanidad*. It is because of the quality and diversity of these last works that the decade of the 1950s stands out as the richest period for twentieth-century architecture in Cuba. In the forefront, and prefiguring much of this work, is the architecture of Eugenio Batista (1900–1992, no relation to the dictator). Batista's work is characterized by a highly sensitive, abstract incorporation of colonial precedents into a modern rendition. The Casa Falla Bonet (1939), with its abstract cubic forms, floating stair and pool that seems to disappear into the ocean on the horizon, anticipates the work of Luis

Eugenio Batista, Casa Falla Bonet, 1939

TOP LEFT: *Moenck y Quintana, Cabana of the Hotel Kawama, 1955* (SERVIFOTO)
TOP CENTER: *Moenck y Quintana, Casa Ramirez Corría, 1956* (SERVIFOTO)
TOP RIGHT: *Mario Romañach, Casa Alvarez, 1957* (SERVIFOTO)
BOTTOM LEFT: *Manuel Gutiérrez, Casa Verdera, 1955* (JOHN A. LOOMIS)
BOTTOM RIGHT: *Fernando Salinas, Casa Higinio Miguel, 1958* (JOHN A. LOOMIS)

Barragán by more than a decade. Batista's own house (1944) is characterized by a subtle appropriation of colonial massing, distinct relationships
between solids and voids, spareness of detail, and a manipulation of the
section that recalls the work of Adolf Loos.

Other significant architects who explored the realm of *cubanidad* in
residential architecture included Nicolás Quintana (b. 1925), Frank
Martínez (b. 1924), Silverio Bosch (b. 1918) and Mario Romañach
(1917–1984), Emilio del Junco (1915–1974), Manuel Gutiérrez (b. 1925),
and Fernando Salinas (1930–1993). Quintana developed a modern idiom
informed by responses to the tropical environment that exhibit a clarity of
structure and lightness of mass as seen in the cabanas of the Hotel
Kawama (1955). In his Casa Ramirez Corría (1956), a series of courtyards
within a walled compound provide cross ventilation for all rooms, elabo-
rating a Spanish-Moorish tradition within a modern syntax. The work of
Bosch and Romañach also represents a regionalist reelaboration of modernist themes, such as the Casa Noval (1949), a bar hovering above the
ground plane on pilotis and punctured by a void providing a shady gathering place; and the Casa Aristigueta (1953) which represents more of an
integration with the landscape. The work of Frank Martínez reflects both
the massing of colonial precedents as well as sedate typological reinterpre-
tations of courtyards, balconies and other elements as seen in much of his
residential work. Likewise, Emilio del Junco's own house (1957), in an
extreme departure from his International Style commercial work, draws
from colonial precedents, but of a more rustic vernacular origin. By contrast, the Casa Alvarez (1957), by Mario Romañach (without Bosch)

ABOVE LEFT: *Quintana, Rubio y Pérez, Medical Offices, 1953-54 (SERVIFOTO)*
ABOVE CENTER: *Gustavo Moreno López, Misiones Office Building, 1951-52 (SERVIFOTO)*
ABOVE RIGHT: *Capablanca y Graupera, Tribunal de Cuentas, 1952-54 (C. ARIAS)*
RIGHT: *Max Borges, Jr., Sala Arcos de Cristal, Cabaret Tropicana, 1952 (COURTESY MAX BORGES JR.)*

exhibits a dynamic relationship of shifting volumes and planes that bear some similarities to Rudolph Schindler and de Stijl, representing one of the most original works of this period. Manuel Gutiérrez's work of this period exhibits highly creative and economical structural propositions such as the undulating ferrocement roof of the Casa Verdera (1955). Fernando Salinas, newly returned from having worked in New York on the Seagram's Building for Mies van der Rohe, demonstrated a Wrightian inclination in the Casa Higinio Miguel (1958).[13] This body of work demonstrates that Cuba was developing a distinctly creative, critical, and regional presence within the waning years of the Modern Movement.

However, little of the work that represented the avant garde of Cuban architecture and *cubanidad* was celebrated in the Museum of Modern Art's 1954 exhibit and catalogue, *Latin American Architecture Since 1945*, curated and written by Henry-Russell Hitchcock.[14] Hitchcock selected: office buildings by Antonio Quintana (1953–54) and Gustavo Moreno (1951–52), typical and not particularly remarkable commercial developments; the aforementioned U.S. Embassy (1952–53) by non-Cubans Harrison and Abramowitz, a rather somber testimony to U.S. hegemony on the island; and the Tribunal de Cuentas (1952–54) by Aquiles Capablanca, a carefully proportioned and detailed Corbusian government ministry building, with a mural by Amelia Peláez, that is often compared to Oscar Niemeyer's Ministry of Education (1937–42) in Rio de Janeiro. In sharp contrast to these rationalist, and not unpredictable, examples of modernism in the MoMA exhibit stood the Cabaret Tropicana (1952) by Max Borges, Jr. (b. 1918). In the Sala Arcos de Cristal of Borges's nightclub, the organic, episodic nature of the plan, the filtered light, integration with the landscape, and the arched thin-shell construction would be an interesting reference point for the National Art Schools a decade later. While acknowledging some Cuban contributions to modern architecture, Hitchcock nevertheless seemed more intent on revalidating his (and Philip Johnson's) own vision of the International Style rather than demonstrating the diversity and richness of Cuban modern architecture.

Within this lively cultural atmosphere of the 1950s, the young Ricardo Porro (b. 1925) began to emerge as an important figure. Having graduated in architecture from the University of Havana in 1949, he had returned in 1952 after two years of postgraduate studies at the Institute of Urbanism at the Sorbonne in Paris. While in Paris he spent much time with expatriate painter Wifredo Lam, whom he credits for having had a great influence on him in terms of both art and politics, for it was Lam who early on converted him to Marxism. Porro also made the acquaintance of Pablo Picasso, and on his travels visited the works of Gunnar Asplund, whose command of plastic forms deeply impressed him. Before Porro's return to Cuba he attended a course in Venice organized by CIAM that was taught by, among others, Le Corbusier, Giulio Carlo Argan, Ignacio Gardella, Ernesto Rogers, Carlo Scarpa, and Bruno Zevi. Rogers's theoretical ideas concerning tradition and historical continuity had a genuine resonance with the debate that had been occurring back in Cuba.

Upon his return to Cuba, Porro worked for others and began to build his own architectural practice, consisting of residential works in Havana's affluent suburbs. He also took a brief trip to Mexico, where he encountered the work and person of Luis Barragán. Porro's work evolved from a Miesian rationalism informed by the tropical climate, as exhibited in the Casa Armenteros (1949) and Casa García (1953), toward a much more organic and personal expression of form, as seen in the Casa Villegas (1954) and Casa Ennis (1957). Porro was very much a participant in the cultural life of this period, as the architect and painter Hugo Consuegra explained:

> Ricardo Porro assumed a very provocative role in Cuban culture during these years. . . . Porro proposed the heresy of organic architecture. He gave lectures at the Colegio de Arquitectos and incessantly proselytized to anyone who would listen. During these years Porro was enlightened—he radiated energy. His friends were painters, musicians, filmmakers, and writers, and he made

LEFT: *Ricardo Porro, Casa García, 1953* (JOHN A. LOOMIS)
RIGHT: *Ricardo Porro, Casa Ennis, 1957* (UNKNOWN PHOTOGRAPHER)

himself heard in all the intellectual circles of Havana. It became quite the fashion to talk about Porro. His sermons contradicted the latest wave of the avant garde, making many of the young feel prematurely old fashioned. All of a sudden Gropius, Neutra, and Mies were ancient history. Porro respected Le Corbusier only because of Ronchamp but would have nothing to do with the "machine for living." He accused Mario Romañach, Tonino Quintana, Frank Martínez, Humberto Alonso, Emilio del Junco, and all the other Cuban "modernos" of being passé. He had no fear of attacking our own sacred cows.[15]

Porro outlined his position in a thoughtful analysis entitled "El sentido de la tradición," published in 1957.[16] In it he discussed the twofold challenge facing the socially committed architect: first, that the architectural work have social merit, and second that it reflect Cuban tradition. He went on to state that the existing political and economic conditions made the first goal impossible to achieve, so the conscientious architect could only, and therefore must, strive to achieve the second through a selective and nonliteral interpretation of history. He singled out the work of Eugenio Batista as being the most successful in synthesizing *arquitectura criolla* and modernism. The discourse on *cubanidad* in architecture, as exemplified by Batista's work, had by and large been framed by the Creole intellectual tendency of the previous decades. While Porro acknowledged the importance of Cuba's *arquitectura criolla*, he made a clear distinction between it and Spanish architecture, which he characterized as embodying the severity of Catholic Spain. Porro recognized that Cuba's culture had been profoundly affected by the culture and especially religion of the African diaspora, resulting in a Cuba that was really not all that Catholic. He asserted that the formal differences between Cuba's *arquitectura criolla* and Spanish architecture were a result of the softening influence of African culture. In a few years he would adopt a more strongly *negrista* position, declaring "*Cuba es una mulata,*" and calling for "*una arquitectura negra.*"

Revolution

This intellectual environment of architectural inquiry in 1950s Cuba was taking place during the repressive regime of the dictator Fulgencio Batista. Arquitectos Unidos themselves came under investigation by the BRAC (Bureau de Represión de Actividades Comunistas), and they were forced to suspend their "salons" in 1955, though remaining professionally active until 1956. In December of that year the guerrilla forces of the July 26th Movement, led by Fidel Castro, began their armed opposition to the Batista government in the eastern Sierra Maestra far away from Havana. Concurrent with the growing political turmoil was a booming economy fed largely by foreign (U.S.) capital. A majority of banks, public services, sugar plantations, and industries were foreign-owned. On the outside, Havana's character was that of a well-appointed Caribbean resort for North Americans. But on the inside, political corruption and economic disparities were provoking a national crisis.[17] Porro remarks today that building and real-estate development in El Vedado was nothing more than "*cocacolonialismo*." But this did not matter for the majority of Cuban architects involved in private practice, 90% of whom practiced in Havana and represented an older and established generation. For them, times were prosperous. For the younger generation who engaged in the oppositional intellectual and political activities, uncertainty or even danger threatened. Architecture students and recent graduates, such as Osmany Cienfuegos (brother of guerrilla leader Camilo Cienfuegos), Mario Coyula Cowley, Selma Díaz, Emilio Escobar Loret de Mola, Josefina Rebellón, Fernando Salinas, and others were very active in anti-Batista activities. One young architecture student, José Antonio Echeverría, a leader of the Directorio Revolucionario, was killed in an incident related to the abortive assault on the Presidential Palace on March 13, 1957.

Ricardo Porro's opposition to the Batista dictatorship led to his involvement in the Movimiento de Resistencia Cívica. His home became a safe house for those working in the underground resistance. Carlos Rafael Rodríguez, a Communist, and Armando Hart, then very anti-communist, were both close friends of Porro's and frequent visitors. Rodríguez later split from the mainstream Communists, the Partido Socialista Popular (PSP), and aligned himself with the guerrillas in the Sierra Maestra. Hart ended up in prison, and Porro soon was forced into exile. Porro recalls:

> Batista was a wretched one . . . a thief, bloodthirsty—not as bloodthirsty as some others, less perhaps, but in the end . . . I was disgusted, so I did what I could do, I was involved in conspiracies, but I was not a revolutionary with a machine gun; I am just not that type. I could not shoot a gun, much less kill anyone. But I aided the Revolution wherever possible, very modestly. I was on the side of Fidel, I found him very appealing, and the only alternative to the

old regime of corrupt politicians. Besides, at that time, I was a Marxist, as were almost all of the young intellectuals of that time—yes, back then we were all Marxists. I was never a member of the Party, I was a so-called fellow traveler. The Party, like the Catholic church, tried to appear to be in opposition, but it gave no real support to the Revolution. . . . Therefore, I participated in the underground struggle. I tried to help in the general strike, [April 9, 1958] which was a fiasco. After this I learned that the police had been informed of my involvement. So in 1958, I departed for Venezuela.[18]

In Venezuela Porro maintained his characteristically intense level of activity. He worked at the Banco Obrero, a government office of public works charged with much of the country's urban design and social housing. The head of the Banco Obrero was Carlos Raúl Villanueva (1900-1975), master architect of Venezuela's Ciudad Universitaria (1944–60). Sponsored by Villanueva, Porro also began teaching design and theory in the architecture school of the Universidad Central de Caracas. While in Venezuela, Porro met two young Italian architects, Vittorio Garatti, with

Carlos Raúl Villanueva, Ramp from the Aula Magna to the Plaza Cubierta, Ciudad Universitaria, Caracas, 1952-53 (ROLLIE MCKENNA)

whom he worked at the Banco Obrero, and later Roberto Gottardi. The three shared interests in history, politics and the reformulation of contemporary architecture. Caracas had some interesting examples. The space of the curved, ramped lobby of the great hall of Villanueva's Ciudad Universitaria, dappled with light filtered through a lattice wall, was a contemporary icon. Félix Candela (b. 1910) built the plastic forms of the Club Playa Azul (1956). Also, the Club Tachira (1956) by Fruto Vivas (b. 1928) with its hyperbolic paraboloid roof was both spatially and technically avant garde.

A New Start

In August 1960 Porro returned to liberated Cuba to help reconstruct the country at the urging of Osmany Cienfuegos, now the new head of the Ministry of Construction (MICONS). But to remain in Cuba after the victory of the Revolution was an unpopular choice for most of Cuba's established architects. As the capital and class interests they had served came under attack by the emerging political and social program of the new revolution, there was a near mass exodus of a whole generation of Cuban architects. The diaspora included Eugenio Batista, an eponymous move to Eugene, Oregon; Max Borges, Jr. to Virginia; Silverio Bosch to Los Angeles; Emilio del Junco to Toronto; Mario Romañach to academic appointments at Cornell, Harvard, and the University of Pennsylvania; Frank Martínez to Miami; Nicolás Quintana to Caracas, Puerto Rico, and Miami; and many others, who sought to reestablish their careers abroad, though few would again enjoy the degree of success that they had achieved in their own country.[19] One of the few architects of this generation to remain and rise to prominence was the late Antonio Quintana Simonetti (1919–93; no relation to Nicolás). His best work, however, remains that of the 1950s.

The flight of this generation of Cuba's practicing architects was condemned as the betrayal of counterrevolutionaries.[20] Their work inevitably became considered somewhat guilty by association, and came to be denied or treated in a cursory fashion in courses on architectural history. The impressive architectural achievements of this lost generation of prerevolutionary Cuba are now being recovered and reevaluated through the efforts of Eduardo Luis Rodríguez and other Cuban historians. Nevertheless, at that time, the departure of Cuba's most important practitioners would cause a major break in the continuity of architectural development in the country which had many building needs with which to contend.

The departure of so many architects affected education too, requiring the restructuring of the faculty of the architecture school, located still in the University of Havana in El Vedado. This opened up opportunities for young professors and recent graduates, though this process was not without conflict as Hugo Consuegra recalls:

> The year 1959 had been chaotic for the school: professors expelled, professors exiled, underenrolled classes, disoriented students, incomplete programs. Some diplomas were conferred under pressure to students for their "revolutionary" credentials. Others plodded through the traditional path: analytic geometry, calculus, statics, structures, etc.[21]

In September of 1960 Consuegra, with Fernando Salinas and Raúl González met to reorganize the program. They invited to join the faculty Ricardo Porro, who had just returned from Venezuela, and the Spanish architect, Joaquín Rallo, who had come from Philadelphia where he had worked for Louis Kahn. A few months later, Vittorio Garatti and Roberto Gottardi also joined. Artists Raúl Martínez, Guido Llinás, Tomás Oliva and Loló Soldevilla were also added to the staff of motivated and talented young professors intent on redirecting architectural education in revolutionary Cuba.[22]

"Notwithstanding the political violence and the difficulty of change, the 1960s was a time of cultural splendor during which a plurality of artistic tendencies flourished," states art critic Gerardo Mosquera.[23] Indeed, in contrast to the departure of Cuba's prominent architects, many prominent artists and intellectuals who had spent the Batista years abroad now returned, initiating a period of energetic artistic activity. Alicia Alonso returned from the New York City Ballet to found the National Ballet of

Cuba. Alejo Carpentier, Nicolás Guillén and Heberto Padilla returned to write. Wifredo Lam, without altogether abandoning his Paris residence, nevertheless came to spend more time working in Cuba. Other cultural figures such as writers Edmundo Desnoes, José Lezama Lima, Virgilio Piñera, José Alvarez Baragaño, and painter René Portocarrero, who had remained in Cuba, joined forces to create a new revolutionary culture. New publications such as the feisty *Lunes de Revolución*, edited by Guillermo Cabrera Infante, promoted provocative literary works and criticism. A number of artistic and literary salons spontaneously enlivened the cultural environment. Virgilio Piñera and José Lezama Lima had their followers, along with other informal groups led by Olga Andreu, María Maya Surduts and later Wanda Garatti, and not without a certain amount of rivalry. Several women also emerged as important official cultural leaders: Vincentina Antuña, the director of the National Council for Culture; Edith García Buchaca, who as the PSP's political liason to the National Council of Culture, wielded equal or greater power; Marta Arjona, a PSP member, ceramic artist, and Director of Plastic Arts within the National Council of Culture; Haydée Santamaría, head of Casa de las Américas; and Celia Sánchez, secretary and confidante of Fidel Castro.[24] Of emerging importance was a young protégé of García Buchaca, Selma Díaz, who would be instrumental in promoting Ricardo Porro for the commission of the National Art Schools. While the early years of the revolutionary government were characterized by this burst of creative activity and utopian optimism that energized culture and expanded the intellectual discourse on *cubanidad*, foundations would also be laid for sectarian politics that would eventually undermine the careers of some of the Cuban Revolution's best and brightest.[25] Nevertheless, these early years are remembered by the enthusiasm and optimism they inspired, as Roberto Gottardi recalls:

> I remember the first years of the Revolution with much nostalgia. The spirit in which one worked was very beautiful. In a certain sense, we had much freedom. There was an atmosphere in which one thought, one reflected. I have never since had an opportunity to engage in a project of this type. To found a new country, with a new people, was a great undertaking.[26]

NOTES

1. "Sin el negro Cuba no sería Cuba," Fernando Ortiz Fernández. *Miscelenea II of Studies Dedicated to Fernano Ortiz* (New York: Interamericas, 1998), 39.
2. For a further discussion of race and identity in Cuba, see Darién J. Davis, "¿Criollo o Mulato? Cultural Identity in Cuba, 1930–1960," in *Ethnicity, Race and Nationality in the Caribbean: The African Impact on Latin America and the Caribbean*, Juan Manuel Carrion, ed. (San Juan: Institute of Caribbean Studies, 1997), 69–95.
3. Narciso Menocal, "An Overriding Passion—The Quest for a National Identity in Painting," *The Journal of Decorative and Propaganda Arts, Cuba Theme Issue* (1996): 187.
4. Alfred H. Barr Jr., "Modern Cuban Painters," *Museum of Modern Art Bulletin* I (1944): 2–14.
5. Gerardo Mosquera, "Modernism from Afro-America: Wifredo Lam," in Mosquera, ed. *Beyond the Fantastic, Contemporary Art Criticism from Latin America* (London: Institute of International Visual Arts, 1995), 120, 130. Two additional useful sources for art history in Cuba are Narciso Menocal, op. cit., and Giulio Blanc and Gerardo Mosquera, "Cuba 1950–1995," in Edward J. Sullivan, ed., *Latin American Art in the Twentieth Century* (London: Paidon Press, 1996).
6. Joaquín Weiss y Sánchez, *Arquitectura cubana colonial* (Havana: Cultural S.A., 1936), republished as *La arquitectura colonial cubana* (Havana: Instituto Cubano del Libro, 1979) and as *La Arquitectura Colonial Cubana, Siglos XVI al XIX* (Sevilla: Junta de Andalucía, 1997).
7. Nancy Stout and Jorge Rigau, *Havana* (New York: Rizzoli, 1994), 55.
8. Francisco Prat Puig, *El prebarroco en Cuba—una escuela criolla de arquitectura morisca* (Havana: Burgay y CIA, 1947).
9. Eugenio Batista, Miguel Gastón, Nicolás Arroyo, Gabriela Menéndez, Manuel de Tapia Ruano, Carlos Alzogaray, Beatríz Masó, and Rita Gutiérrez, were all founding members of ATEC.
10. Ricardo Porro recounts an amusing story regarding Philip Johnson's unsuccessful attempt to develop a hotel and casino project for Meyer Lansky and Co. in 1956. Having just been retained by his new clients, Johnson traveled to Havana with a small entourage that included Phyllis Lambert for his first meeting. There he engaged as his local architects del Junco, Gastón y Domínguez, at whose office Porro was employed, and became Johnson's personal assistant. In an early meeting with Johnson, Porro suggested that in the spirit of *cubanidad,* the lobby of the casino have a large mural by Wifredo Lam, an idea that met with Johnson's enthusiasm. But it all was to unravel at the first meeting with the clients. At this time in Cuba, businessmen uniformly wore white linen suits, with white starched shirts and cream colored Panama hats. Johnson, with an appropriately attired Porro, showed up for the meeting dressed in black suit, black shirt, black tie and signature black Corbu glasses. As the meeting progressed, Johnson presented the idea for the mural by Lam. One of the gangster types responded, "I tink dat is a very good idear. It should be like two big dice hanging over all da people's heads." After a pause, Johnson replied coolly, "Gentlemen, let us not be vulgar." A silence followed. The meeting abruptly ended.
11. Nicolás Arroyo, Eugenio Batista, Rita Gutiérez, Gabriela Menéndez, and Nicolás Quintana were among these architects.
12. The group included Hugo Consuegra, Sergio González, Henry Gutiérrez, Manolo Mesa, Serafín Miguenes, Vicente Morales, Urcesino Otero, Pablo Pérez, and Osvaldo Tapia Ruano. Many of the architects, artists, writers, and filmmakers who participated in the weekly salons went on to assume positions of ministerial or academic importance within the Revolution or to roles of prominence as dissident intellectuals in exile. Among these included José Alvarez Baragaño, Hugo D'Acosta, Edmundo Desnoes, Osmany Cienfuegos, Guido Llinás, Tomás Oliva, Nicolás Quintana, Antonio Quintana, Alberto Robaina, Fernando Salinas, and Severo Sarduy.
13. For further information on the architecture of this period, see Nicolás Quintana, "Evolución Histórica de la Arquitectura en Cuba—Epoca Republicana (1900–1959)," *La Enciclopedia de Cuba* (San Juan: Enciclopedia y Clásicos Cubanos, 1977), as well as Eduardo Luis Rodríguez, *La Habana Arquitectura del Siglo XX* (Barcelona: Editorial Blume, 1998) and Roberto Segre, "As Formulaçaõs Teóricas na Década de 50," *America Latina Fim de Milénio* (São Paolo: Studio Nobel, 1991), 24–36.
14. Henry-Russell Hitchcock, *Latin American Architecture Since 1945* (New York: Museum of Modern Art, 1955), 55, 72–75, 108–109, 194.
15. Hugo Consuegra, unpublished memoirs.
16. Ricardo Porro, "El sentido de la tradición," *Nuestro Tiempo* 16, año IV (1957) (author's translation). See "Documents" for a translated excerpt.
17. The world of prerevolutionary Havana is vividly described in Graham Greene's *Our Man in Havana* (London: Heinemann Ltd., 1958).
18. R. Porro., interview with the author (July 1992).

It is interesting to note that the Partido Socialista Popular (PSP, as Cuba's Communist party was then called) was for a long time quite ambivalent in its support of the armed struggle fomented by the July 26th Movement. In fact it actually condemned the 1953 assault on the Moncada barracks as an "adventurist" action. Walterio Carbonell, a historian, ethnologist and one of the Party's few Afro-Cuban members, was expelled for expressing his support for Fidel Castro and the other imprisoned attackers. It was not until after the victory that the PSP's participation in the Cuban Revolution began to gain significance. Subsequent negotiations and struggles between the leaderships of the PSP, the July 26th Movement, and the Directorio Revolucionario would shape the future Communist Party of Cuba and consolidate power in the hands of Fidel Castro and others. Recalcitrant old-line party members such as Aníbal Escalante would be sent on "extended vacation" to Moscow or even imprisoned. When the Cuban Communist Party's first Politburo was founded in 1965, not one old-time member of the PSP, with the exception of Carlos Rafael Rodríguez, was found among its membership.

19. The story of this architectural diaspora is currently a subject of research by Cuban architect, historian, and Guggenheim Fellow, Eduardo Luis Rodríguez.

20. Not to say that some did not actually actively seek to overthrow the new government. Che Guevara's confrontation with Nicolás Quintana over his clandestine counterrevolutionary activities is an interesting anecdote. See John Lee Anderson, *Che Guevara, a Revolutionary Life* (New York: Grove Press, 1997), 458–59.

21. Hugo Consuegra, unpublished memoirs (author's translation).

22. The fate of many of these idealistic young men was unfortunate. Porro resigned from the faculty in 1963 after repeated conflicts with Salinas. Llinás departed for Paris, also in 1963. Oliva and Soldevilla were eased out for their "formalist" and "intellectual" orientations. Martínez was expelled in a purge of homosexuals in 1965. Consuegra resigned from the faculty in 1966 and subsequently left the country. Salinas himself was removed in 1965. Rallo died tragically of a heart attack in 1967, working far away in Jagüey Grande, under difficult conditions imposed upon him to rectify his "bourgeois" orientation. Garatti was forced to leave the country in 1974.

23. Gerardo Mosquera, "Cuba, 1950–1995," Edward J. Sullivan, ed., *Latin American Art in the Twentieth Century* (London: Phaidon Press, 1996), 92.

24. These intellectual, cultured, and revolutionary women were almost all connected to politically powerful men: Edith García Buchaca's husband, Joaquín Ordoqui, was a government minister who, like herself, was a veteran member of the PSP. Haydée Santamaría was married to Armando Hart, a revolutionary leader who became minister of education and later culture. Celia Sánchez was intimately involved with Fidel Castro. Selma Díaz was married to Osmany Cienfuegos, who became director of the Ministry of Construction.

25. The ultimate destinies of these cultural figures are quite diverse, as some of the following illustrate. Alicia Alonso continues to direct and dance in the National Ballet of Cuba. Alejo Carpentier and Nicolás Guillen lived out their lives as Cuba's literary laureates. Heberto Padilla, Guillermo Cabrera Infante, and much later, Edmundo Desnoes chose exile. Vincentina Atuña quietly lived out the rest of her life in retirement in Havana. Edith García Buchaca fell from grace, following a political trial, and died in 1979 after fifteen years of house arrest. Olga Andreu, and later Haydée Santamaría, committed suicide. María Maya Surduts left for France where she became a leader in the women's movement. Wanda Garatti returned to her native Italy with her husband, Vittorio, following his expulsion in 1974. Marta Arjona, as Director of Cultural Patrimony, and Selma Díaz, as Director of Habitat Cuba, continue to be highly regarded cultural figures in Cuba today.

26. Roberto Gottardi, interview with the author (June 1992).

. . . revolutions have their utopian period, in

which their protagonists, committed to the

noble duty of transforming their dreams into

reality and putting into practice their ideals,

believe that the historical goals are much

closer than they are in reality, and that their

will, their desires and their intentions, above

and beyond all objective facts, are omnipotent.

Fidel Castro

T W O

Founding the Schools

One late afternoon in January 1961, an unlikely pair of golfers, Fidel Castro and Che Guevara, enjoyed a few rounds on the well-manicured course of what had been the exclusive country club of Havana's elite. There they pondered the future of this unique site for a new society, in which exclusive country clubs would have no place. The beautifully landscaped country club was the crown jewel in Havana's most affluent suburb, aptly named Country Club Park. Laid out in 1914, it was mostly developed in the 1920s and 1930s at the far western reaches of the city, near "whites only" beaches and the Yacht Club. Breaking with the traditional Spanish grid patterns of Havana's other neighborhoods, the meandering Garden City drives of Country Club Park set it apart from the rest of the city. But with the Revolution most of its inhabitants fled, and the area was renamed Cubanacán, a name from Cuba's indigenous past. Though many residences were reserved for members of the new leadership as well as for foreign diplomats, Cubanacán's beaches to the north of the club were now open to the general public and the whole, formerly private, preserve was to be devoted to social uses, with the former country club occupying a central place. Surveying the immaculate golf course and surrounding woods, the two former guerrilla leaders, now responsible for developing and executing social and cultural policy, came upon the idea of creating an innovative school of the arts.

Education was conceived as the fulcrum around which the Cuban Revolution's economic, political, social and cultural programs would revolve. On January 1 a National Literacy Campaign had been launched, sending 235,000 volunteers throughout the country. In the course of just one year they would reduce the country's illiteracy rate from 25% to 3.9%. The revolutionary leaders wanted to capitalize upon this wave of popular mobilization and education. Ideas were circulating as to how to extend this momentum to the promotion of cultural activities. It was a visionary moment for the new revolution, with the literacy campaign just underway, when the idea for the art schools was launched. The newly formed board

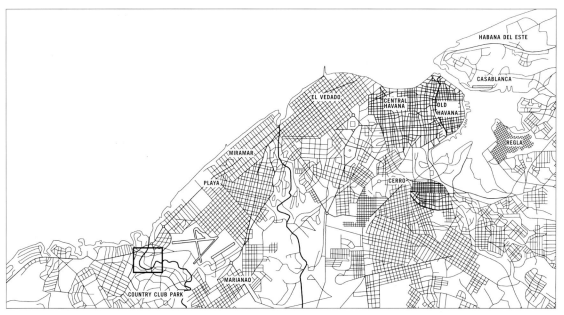

Schematic plan of Havana, with site for the National Art Schools in
Country Club Park outlined at lower left (WILLIAM DUNCANSON)

of the schools, drew up a program that would serve Cubans as a center
for the education of artists and instructors from which to disseminate cultural literacy throughout the island. But in response to Che Guevara's
internationalist interests, the program would extend beyond that and
also serve as an international center, primarily drawing from the Third
World, granting full scholarships to some three thousand students from
Africa, Asia and Latin America in the service of the creation of a "new
culture" for the "new man." The political objective of the schools would
be to educate those artists who would give socialism in both Cuba and
the Third World its aesthetic representation. Moreover, the schools were
conceived as an experimental center for intercultural education and
exchange. Since the idea and the site were without precedent, it was
decided that the architecture, too, should be without precedent. The
visionary spirit in which the program was conceived would be symbolized
in its design. Carlos Rafael Rodríguez, Cuba's late Vice President, recalls
the act of founding the schools:

> I remember vividly today that afternoon when compañero Fidel Castro, from
> one of these balconies, accompanied by compañero Hart and some others of
> us, sketched out what was to become the National Art Schools. The place had
> been, up to a short time before, where both Cuban and foreign aristocrats
> would meet in its exclusive confines to enjoy their prosperity derived from the
> extortion of our people and the exploitation of our wealth. In what had been
> their favorite golf course, in this beautiful setting, our Secretary General, with
> that creative imagination for which he is known, outlined for us what would

be the image of this new incubator of culture, this new school. And because of the unique features of this site, it was agreed by all, that the school should not be like any ordinary school, for it is precisely because this site and its unique features invite a design appropriate to this environment which should become the fountain of our future artists, the creators or interpreters of tomorrow's socialism. And so emerged the beginnings of the foundation of the material support for these beautiful buildings by Cuban and foreign architects. So would begin to develop the dream of that afternoon.[1]

The unique qualities of the site and the program demanded a unique vision, and no one was more appropriate for the commission than Ricardo Porro. Newly returned from Venezuela in August 1960, Porro had been occupied with urban planning up until the moment he received the commission for the schools. Even though it was Fidel Castro who would personally give Ricardo Porro "the command" of planning the schools in January 1961, the offer was brought to him by his old friend from university days, Selma Díaz, whose husband was Osmany Cienfuegos, the twenty-five-year-old head of the Ministry of Construction (MICONS).

> There was a cocktail party at my house. Selma Díaz showed up (uninvited) and told me she had a proposal direct from Fidel, that he wanted to create a school of the arts in what had been the country club and that he wanted it to be unlike any other. She said that Fidel wanted its architecture to be completely new and that it should be the most beautiful school ever, and Selma said that he expected them to be complete in two months. I said that this would be impossible. But she replied that this was Fidel's proposal and I could take it or leave it. So I did what any architect would do, I said yes, of course I would take it.[2]

It was not out of character for Porro to agree to the impossible. Ricardo Porro Hidalgo, who likes to point out that he was born the year before Fidel Castro, 1925, once said, "It has been claimed that my pride is greater than my intelligence, no mean measure in my unhumble opinion."[3] Gilberto Seguí, who worked as a young draftsman under Porro on the National Art Schools, describes his acquaintance with Porro:

> . . . the Revolution had triumphed. All our hopes had been raised. Utopia, everything seemed possible, in politics as well as in architecture. . . [Ricardo Porro] gave a series of lectures at the National Library, each one dedicated to a different architect: Mies van der Rohe, Le Corbusier, Alvar Aalto and finally—Frank Lloyd Wright. Porro used an unknown language. He spoke of art, of poetry. I remember the emotion he aroused in the room when he declared himself a Marxist. . . . I introduced myself to Porro one day as we

"The Plastic [Organic] Movement from World War II to Today," *poster for three lectures by Ricardo Porro, 1961*

both happened to be on the number 22 bus going toward Marianao. I still remember the welcoming atmosphere of his house in the La Sierra neighborhood, where he lived with his wife and their little boy, surrounded by paintings of Lam, of Milián and ceramics by Picasso. Some of the neighbors were scandalized by Lam's paintings, believing that they were objects of sorcery! Porro had just been put in charge of the project for the National Art Schools at Cubanacán. I saw his first sketches. He had produced an architecture of fantasy, with many elements of *cubanidad* and others non-Cuban, but for me they were only comparable with the works I had seen in photos and drawings of Wright. I was enthusiastic, and right away I requested authorization to work with him.[4]

The schools were conceived at an inspired moment. Porro recalls it in terms of almost magic realism as "the moment, common to every revolution, during which the marvelous becomes the everyday and the Revolution appeared—*más surrealista que socialista.*"[5] To symbolically connect the new cultural program with the unfolding success of the literacy campaign, government officials now imposed a less unreasonable but still demanding deadline for the inauguration of the schools: the official end of the literacy campaign, December 22, 1961. Porro knew he could not accomplish the task alone. To collaborate on the project he called upon architect Iván Espín, brother-in-law of Raúl Castro, and his Italian colleagues from Venezuela, Roberto Gottardi and Vittorio Garatti. (Espín dropped out early on in the collaboration.) Part of a small but dedicated international community of architects[6] who had come to contribute their professional skills to the Cuban Revolution, Gottardi and Garatti had arrived in December 1960 and were working in physical planning when Porro invited them to join him on the project for the National Art Schools.

Gottardi and Garatti brought their own unique talents and experiences to the project. Both had been exposed to postwar antirationalist currents in Italy prior to coming to Cuba. The revisionist thought of Ernesto Nathan Rogers had been an important influence on each of them. Garatti's and Gottardi's exposure to alternatives to the Modern Movement, proposed in the critical architectural environment of 1950s Italy, created a sympathetic bond with Porro, who also brought to the project his ongoing search for an authentic architectural *cubanidad.*

Roberto Gottardi, born 1927 in Venice, studied architecture at the Instituto Superiore di Architettura di Venezia where both Bruno Zevi and Carlo Scarpa were influential. He had the good fortune of being one of Scarpa's students prior to his graduation in 1952. Gottardi credits Scarpa as an important influence on his own approach to design:

LEFT: *Ricardo Porro* (PAOLO GASPARINI)
CENTER: *Ernesto Rogers and Roberto Gottardi* (UNKNOWN PHOTOGRAPHER)
RIGHT: *Vittorio Garatti seated on Havana's Malecon* (UNKNOWN PHOTOGRAPHER)

Scarpa is the teacher who influenced me the most. He taught me much about architecture as well as about many other things. For me the experience with Scarpa was not about formal codes. It was more about the manner in which to pose a problem and how to think about architecture—something very indirect. Every time I go to Venice, I search out his work and I always learn something new.[7]

From 1956 to 1957, Gottardi had worked closely with Ernesto Rogers in the studio Banfi, Belgiojoso, Peressuti, Rogers (BBPR). This environment where theory and practice converged would also be an important part of his formation. In November 1957 upon the invitation of a Venezuelan architect visiting Rogers, Gottardi left for Maracaibo. He later moved to Caracas, where a mutual friend, the photographer Paolo Gasparini, introduced him to Vittorio Garatti and later to Ricardo Porro.

Vittorio Garatti, born 1927 in Milan, graduated from the Politécnico di Milano in 1957 where Rogers taught and where among his classmates were Gae Aulenti and Guido Canela. He left that same year for Caracas with his wife to join his parents and siblings who had immigrated there in 1948. There, after other jobs, he found employment in the Banco Obrero where he befriended Ricardo Porro. Porro provided Garatti an introduction to the university, where he also taught until 1960 when he decided to commit himself to building the Cuban Revolution. Prior to assuming his new responsibilities in Havana, Garatti and his wife took a fifteen-day trip to the United States, where he sought out the work of Frank Lloyd Wright in Chicago, Racine, and New York. Wright's work deeply impressed him, especially the Johnson Wax Building, and further reinforced his convictions about the deficiencies of International Style modernism.

Porro, Gottardi, and Garatti began to work on the design of the schools in earnest in late April 1961 after the successfully repelled invasion at Playa Girón (Bay of Pigs) earlier that month. The band of fifteen hundred American-backed counterrevolutionaries had been easily defeated by the revolutionary armed forces commanded by Fidel Castro himself. This victory added to the confidence and optimism of the population that supported the Revolution, and reinforced a general feeling of omnipotence. The three architects, themselves energized by the collective euphoria, labored in a commandeered chapel that had once served the aristocratic Sarrá family at their former residence in El Vedado, and which was now the headquarters for the National Council for Culture under the directorship of Vincentina Atuña and the powerful influence of Edith García Buchaca. Important cultural figures such as Alejo Carpentier and Wifredo Lam frequently dropped in to visit the surreal environment of the chapel/design studio, where the country club of Havana's elite was being transformed into art schools for the children of the workers. As Porro recalls:

> I organized our office in the chapel. It was an marvelous place. To work in the chapel was enchanting. A series of delightful youngsters from the architecture school came to help too. I began to work, Vittorio began to work, and Roberto began to work also. And to work in that dark atmosphere, all night and all day, was a poetic experience, the most beautiful possible. It was clear that the architecture we developed right from the beginning was strongly connected to that of each other, even though I did not intervene in the architecture of the others and they did not intervene in mine. . . . *Era una arquitectura rica—orgánica.*[8]

The three architects originally conceived the project as a single center with shared services for five schools: Modern Dance, Plastic Arts, Dramatic Arts, Music, and Ballet.[9] But the directors of the schools soon requested that the individual disciplines be accommodated in separate buildings. This generated a new master plan. Besides assuming general leadership, Porro took responsibility for the design of Modern Dance and Plastic Arts, delegating Gottardi for Dramatic Arts and Garatti for Music and Ballet.

While they worked independently, they agreed that the design of the schools would be governed by three guiding principles that would unify their work. First, the schools were to respect and respond to the verdant landscape of the former country club. The well-manicured golf course occupied the central part of the site, traversed by the Rio Quibú, a small tributary of the Rio Almendares. Therefore, the architects decided to place the individual schools at various locations at the periphery. Modern Dance was placed on a high point overlooking the others. Dramatic Arts was located in the meadow at the edge of the valley, while Ballet was immersed

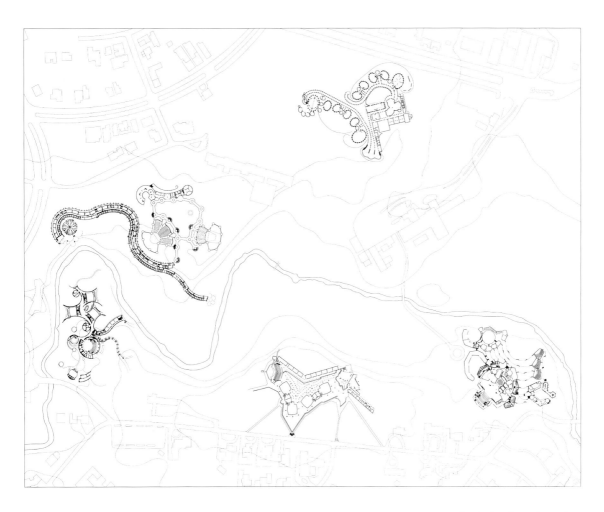

Site plan of the National Art Schools. CLOCKWISE FROM LOWER LEFT: *School of Ballet, School of Music, School of Plastic Arts, School of Dramatic Arts, School of Modern Dance* (WILLIAM DUNCANSON)

in a deep gorge. Music was to occupy a middle ground along the side of a ridge. The existing clubhouse located on the plain would accommodate offices, cafeteria and other common services. Across from it and the entrance to the complex was sited Plastic Arts.

The second guiding principle concerned materials. Due to Cuba's industrial underdevelopment, there was no steel produced on the island and very little Portland cement. The imposition of the U.S. economic blockade on October 19, 1960 and the subsequent inflated cost of imported materials left Cubans to their own devices. With this situation, the Ministry of Construction approved the architects' choice to substitue earthen materials for cement. So it was that brick and terra-cotta tiles became the primary materials used in the construction of the schools.

Contingent to the decision to use brick and tiles was the third and most significant principle, formally and tectonically: the *bóveda catalana*,

Detail of end of a Catalan vault, the
School of Ballet (JOHN A. LOOMIS)

the Catalan vault, would be the primary structural system. This came
about in part due to a fortuitous discovery of a skilled mason from
Barcelona who was the son of a mason who had worked with Antoni
Gaudí. This mason, simply known as Gumersindo, had learned the craft
from his father. Despite its name, the exact origins of the Catalan vault (or
"cohesive timbrel arch construction") are unknown, but attributed to
ancient vernacular practice rooted in the Mediterranean countries of
North Africa, Spain, France and Italy, and perfected in Catalonia.[10] The
technique has several merits. The Catalan vault is typically very thin,
deriving its strength not from its mass, but from both its form and its construction. Thin terra cotta tiles, typically 15 x 30 x 2.5 cm, are positioned
flat in at least two layers, one orthogonal, one diagonal, and held together
by a thick bed of mortar, which, making up about half of the mass, results
in what might be considered almost a concrete shell with a tile aggregate.
Structurally monolithic and light in weight, the Catalan vault offers great
latitude as to form since it exerts very little lateral thrust. It can therefore
assume shapes with very little curvature without impairing its structural
integrity. Because of the strength and cohesive nature of their construction,
Catalan vault structures are virtually indestructible and, in fact, difficult
and costly to demolish.[11]

From its existence as an almost lost art, the Catalan vault was revived
in the 1860s in Barcelona, primarily through the work of Rafael Guastavino y Moreno. In the 1870s he moved to the U.S. where with his son
(also named Rafael) he established the Guastavino Fireproof Construction
Company. Together the father and son team built some of the greatest civic
works of the American Beaux Arts by such architects as McKim, Mead &

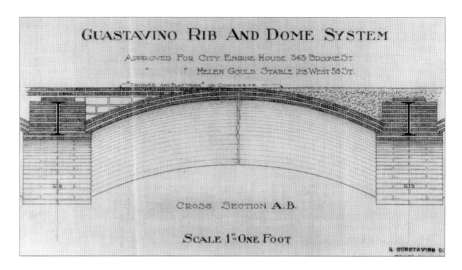

Guastavino Rib and Dome System, Gould Stable and City Engine
House at Broome Street, New York, 1902
(FROM J. PARKS AND A. NEUMANN, THE OLD WORLD BUILDS THE NEW (AVERY LIBRARY, 1996)

White, Richard Morris Hunt, Cass Gilbert, and Carrère & Hastings. The
Boston Public Library, New York's Grand Central Station, Pennsylvania
Station, and the facilities at Ellis Island all incorporate the Guastavinos'
Catalan vault construction. The Guastavinos' greatest structural achievement was the central dome of the Cathedral of St. John the Divine, constructed in 1909 with a diameter of 40.4 m and a crown built of only three
layers of tile, just 11 cm thick. Guastavino the elder also published the first
theoretical treatise on the technique, *Cohesive Construction*, in 1893,
which remains the definitive work on the subject.

While in the U.S. the Catalan vault was a practical solution to structural needs—one most often covered up by neoclassical decoration—in
Barcelona it was loaded with meaning in terms of cultural identity and
was exploited more in terms of its potential for expressive form. Architects
of the Movimento Modernista Catalán, such as Muncunill, Doménech i
Montaner, Puig i Cadafalch and Berenguer, not to mention Antoni Gaudí,
pursued its revival as an assertive plastic expression of cultural and
regional identity. Le Corbusier demonstrated a brief interest in the craft,
incorporating a modified version of it in the roofs of the maisons Jaoul
and Sarabhai. In Argentina both Antoni Bonet and Eduardo Sacriste were
known to have employed it in the 1940s. The Uruguayan engineer Eladio
Dieste, master of plastic form in masonry, used it in many of his unique
projects. The cultural relevance of the craft persisted in Barcelona, where
in 1960, just prior to the National Art Schools, the Church of San Medi by
Jordi Bonet was constructed with hyperbolic paraboloid Catalan vaults.

There are two aspects of the Catalan vault that should be noted. First,
it is a very labor-intensive technique, one requiring skilled masons. For this

reason its use died out in the U.S. during the 1920s and 1930s with the adoption of reinforced concrete. Second, few engineers are familiar with the system or have been capable of providing a quantitative analysis of it, until the more recent development of computerized models. The technique resides within the artisan tradition of the master builder and not within the technical discipline of the engineer.[12] With revolutionary Cuba's material shortages, the use of the Catalan vault was a resourceful and inspired decision. The resulting organic shapes it made possible would be the formal signature of the National Art Schools. Moreover, the cultural significance of the Catalan vault as a craft of Hispanic and Mediterranean origins was well understood by the architects of the National Art Schools, who sought an appropriate idiom in which to develop their vision of a revolutionary *cubanidad*.

In June of 1961, with ground not yet broken and designs still in development, Fidel Castro praised the National Art Schools as "the most beautiful academy of arts in the whole world," and lauded their architects as "artists."[13]

NOTES

1. Carlos Rafael Rodríguez, "Problemas del arte en la Revolución," *Revolución y Cultura* 1, (October 1967): 6, (author's translation). Hart here refers to Armando Hart, the one time anti-communist leader of the Directorio Revolucionario, who after the victory, underwent a dramatic conversion to Marxism and went on to serve as Minister of Education and later of Culture for many years. Carlos Rafael Rodríguez, an old communist from the PSP, who unlike many of his comrades had given his support to the armed struggle early on, held many positions of importance in the government, and served for many years as Vice President. He died in December 1997. Interestingly, this supportive statement was made in 1967, after the "official" repudiation of the schools and Ricardo Porro's departure.

2. R. Porro, interview with the author (November 1997).

3. Nakamura, Toshio, "Ricardo Porro," *A+U* 282 (March 1994): 60.

4. Gilberto Seguí Diviñó, "Les odeurs de la rue," *La Havane 1952-1961, Série Mémoires* 31 (May 1994): 34 (author's translation).

5. R. Porro, "Cinq Aspects du Contenu en Architecture," *PSICON—Rivista Internazionale de Architettura* 2/3 (January/June 1975): 165 (author's translation).

6. Some of the other architects from abroad who came to dedicate their professional skills to the Revolution were: Sergio Baroni (Italy), Rene Du Bois (France), Joaquín Rallo (Spain), Jerry Barr (U.S.), Walter Betancourt (U.S.), Paul Jacobs (U.S.) Roberto Segre (Argentina) and Fruto Vivas (Venezuela). It is interesting to note that Hannes Meyer, Ernst May, Andre Lurçat, and other foreign architects had gone to the Soviet Union in the 1930s, in a parallel act of solidarity, to contribute their skills to the First Five Year Plan.

7. R. Gottardi, interview with the author (June 1992).

8. R. Porro, interview with the author (July 1992).

9. The schools of modern dance and ballet were given separate facilities largely due to the insistence of Alicia Alonso, the prima ballerina and director of the new Cuban National Ballet.

10. For a thorough historical and structural account of the Catalan vault, with particular attention to the work of the Guastavino father-and-son team in the U.S., see George R. Collins, "The Transfer of Thin Masonry Vaulting from Spain to America," *Journal of the Society of Architectural Historians* 27, no. 3 (October 1968): 176-201. Also of interest: Janet Parks and Alan G. Neumann, *The Old World Builds the New: The Guastavino Company and the Technology of the Catalan Vault, 1885-1962* (New York: Columbia University, 1996).

11. "The Metropolitan Museum vaults presented considerable difficulty in their removal. On several visits to the demolition, the present author failed to find a single whole tile in the rubble; the aggregate had proven to be so homogenous and rigid that pneumatic drills were being used with confidence by workers standing on unsupported remnants of the vault that jutted out as much as eight feet." Collins, op. cit., 183.

12. "Such was the case for the Metropolitan Museum of New York in Wings H and E of New York's Metropolitan Museum where cracks developed, apparently from weaknesses of the walls, [built by other contractors] and, as no engineers could be found who could predict reliable enough to satisfy the insurers the action of the existing vaults when submitted to the weight of large exhibition crowds, the Guastavino vaults were removed and replaced with concrete floors." Ibid, n. 11.

13. Fidel Castro Ruz, quoted in "La más hermosa academia de artes de todo el mundo," *Noticias de Hoy*, 4 May 1963 (author's translation). See Documents, herein.

Esta es la nueva escuela, esta es la nueva casa

Casa y escuela nuevas como cuna de una nueva raza.

Silvio Rodríguez

THREE

The National Art Schools

By September 1961 the architects had moved their studio from the chapel to the clubhouse on site in order to be close to the work which had now begun and would proceed on a fast-track basis. The team grew beyond the original architects and their draftsmen to include engineers, plumbers, electricians, and others. They formed a tightly knit interdisciplinary "family" that worked together in what all recall as a festive and spontaneous atmosphere. David Bigelman, a young student draftsman at the time recalls:

> Despite the intense demanding work, the initial conditions were like paradise. The club grounds were beautiful, immaculate. Sometimes for lunch we would even go to the Yacht Club's restaurant. During afternoon break, there was one colleague who would often entertain us with opera arias. And at times, for a lark, we would take the golf carts (which were still working) and race around the site.[1]

The three architects also had other responsibilities. They were designing other projects and competitions, teaching design studios, lecturing and writing curriculum for the restructured architectural school, as well as participating in voluntary work brigades. They involved their students in the design and construction process of the schools, interweaving theory and practice. José Mosquera, a former student of Vittorio Garatti recalls:

> We would spend the mornings at school and the afternoons at the site. Vittorio Garatti was very concerned about the integrative nature of our education and was very dedicated to making the connections between theory and practice. He taught us that the design process eventually generated its own criteria, and once we were integrated with that process, our contributions would be part of that collective whole, not an individual statement. I remember I was given one of the entrances to design while he had gone away for five days. I was very nervous about showing my design to him when he returned. But when I finally showed it to him, he said, "Yes, that is correct. That is the project." And it was built without any changes.[2]

OPPOSITE: *School of Modern Dance, entry, 1965*
(PAOLO GASPARINI)

Students of Vittorio Garatti, 1962.
José Mosquera, center, in glasses
(UNKNOWN PHOTOGRAPHER)

Students affectionately referred to Porro as "Le Porbusier" and "Porromini." He gave lectures on the history of art and architecture to both students and workers during informal gatherings at the site.[3]

One important member of the team was the project's structural engineer, Hilda Fernández, also the young niece of a well-known Cuban engineer. She had been assigned to the project by her superior, Fernando Villa who supported the project but soon left for the United States. Hilda Fernández joined the "family" at Cubanacán in all its work and cultural activities and during the process married one of the foremen.

Clara Porcet was another interesting woman who contributed to the project. Although she was Cuban, she was raised in Mexico where her parents had fled in exile in the 1930s. There she studied design and became acquainted with Luis Barragán, with whom she worked from time to time. Among other things she designed some of the furniture and cabinetry in his house. As a Marxist she was excited by the prospects of the Cuban Revolution and returned to the country of her birth to make her contribution. She worked with Porro, designing all the furniture and cabinetry for both of his schools.

One of the more colorful persons to participate in the project was José Bacallao, the Spanish master mason in charge of the School of Ballet. More than twenty years older than the young architects, he cut a very severe, dignified, figure with old world courtly manners. José Mosquera recalls:

Bacallao was a perfectionist, a very precise man, very Spanish. He had a pole with the standard courses marked out and he would walk around the site, checking on the accuracy of his masons. On at least one occasion he required a mason to completely tear down a wall he had built in the School of Ballet because it did not meet his standards. Bacallao was quite amused at the new

Building a trial Catalan vaulted cupola in the courtyard of the Ministry of Public Works, 1961 (UNKNOWN PHOTOGRAPHER)

situation and at the young architects. He would talk about how before the Revolution, the architect would show up at the site in his white suit, mostly concerned about not getting it dirty. Here Garatti and the others, very informally dressed, were hands-on involved with the workers and treating them as their social equals. He was very happy with this new relationship and he treated the project as a labor of love.[4]

When the masonry was completed on the School of Ballet, José Bacallao retired, believing that he had completed his finest work.

But the real "aristocrat" of the construction crew was Gumersindo. He had come to Cuba from Barcelona to supervise the restoration of a convent. With the Revolution, however, the nuns were expelled, and Gumersindo was left without a job. Fortunately, Porro learned of his situation and engaged him to bring his talents to Cubanacán. Gumersindo was known for his quiet, modest demeanor and for his ability to work for many hours without resting. He began his assignment by training other masons to construct trial Catalan vaults and test them under loads, which they did in the courtyard of the old Ministry of Public Works. In a short time a skilled work force developed—so skilled that at times construction got ahead of design. The construction team exerted considerable pressure on the architects. Drawings were often made in haste, at a small scale with few details—sometimes too late. But the synergy and collaborative spirit between the architects and the builders produced a remarkably unified work. At peak periods of activity there might be as many as three hundred to four hundred workers at each site. To this day the architects speak of the unusual commitment of these workers to the project. This was matched by the students of the future arts schools themselves. With the project still under construction, classes commenced in 1962.[5] As construc-

Site of the School of Ballet in April 1961 (LEFT) *and*
September 1961 (RIGHT) (MICHELENA)

tion proceeded around them, students and teachers developed and put into
practice a highly experimental curriculum that would direct their artistic
formation. While architects, masons, and laborers were toiling, horn play-
ers practiced in the woods and ballet dancers pirouetted on the greens.
There was a passionate sense of ownership and involvement by all—a revolutionary bacchanalia of collective participation. Gottardi remembers:

> The reaction of the workers was interesting. I remember when I first took the
> plans and models to show them and explain the design. I wanted them to
> really participate in what they were building. And with the social changes
> brought by the Revolution it was possible for the workers to think that the
> school that they were building could be for their children. It was not like
> before when they built just for the rich. Their participation, their enthusiasm
> was very important. There were not only close relations between the designers
> and builders but also with the new generation of art students who were there
> from the beginning. They both participated in the shaping of the new curricu-
> lum and the actual building of the schools. There was established a very
> strong relationship among the designers, the builders and these young art stu-
> dents. They too participated in the construction. They helped whether it was
> to build a wall or dig a foundation. At that time voluntary work was very nat-
> ural, very spontaneous with no feeling of obligation.[6]

Garatti recalls:

> The project was accompanied by great enthusiasm. I remember the time when
> it was necessary to pour without interruption the ring of the base of the
> cupola of the main dance pavilion. A party was organized, together with the
> students of the schools, food was distributed so as not to interrupt the work
> and with a group of drummers who played continuous Afro-Cuban rhythms.

To the beat of the congas and with everybody joining in we were able to convince even the truck drivers, who were used to always quitting for their midday meal, to continue to bring concrete to us.[7]

However, there were circumstances beyond the influence of the commitment and enthusiasm of the architects, students and workers. The original internationalist vision for the schools became compromised by international events. The Third World socialist countries had suffered several reversals. The overthrow of Ben Bella removed Algeria from the socialist camp. China's split with the Soviet Union, and Cuba's growing alignment with the USSR, strained relations with that former ally. Vietnam would soon be even more consumed in an escalating war. The ambitious international program for the project was thus scaled down as the schools now officially became known as the National Art Schools. A project with the scope of the arts schools was proving to be an ambitious undertaking for a small country grappling with political and social change, economic hardship, and growing isolation from the international community.

The December 22, 1961 deadline proved unrealizable, though Ricardo Porro's School of Modern Dance and School of Plastic Arts were well advanced. Roberto Gottardi's School of Dramatic Arts went for a period without a director and was dogged by organizational problems as well as lack of a clear program. The faculty was continually changing and so were their requirements for the school. Gottardi was faced with endless programmatic changes, reversals and delays, thus slowing his project's progress. Working closely with Alicia and Fernando Alonso, Vittorio Garatti was able to push ahead the School of Ballet, but his School of Music had a late start. Due to its initial lack of a director, design did not begin until September 1961 and construction not until January 1962. A large concert hall and opera house made it the largest of the five projects. A turning point in the construction of the schools came following the October Crisis (Missile Crisis) of 1962, after which projects not directly involved in economic production were given low priority. The work force began to diminish as the Ministry of Construction redirected workers to other projects deemed of greater importance. As construction gradually lost momentum, the project became paralyzed. Nevertheless, by September 1963, when the UIA held its congress in Havana, the National Arts Schools were well on their way to completion. They received favorable attention from more than twenty-five hundred architects who came to visit the former country club.[8] There was the expectation that the work would resume in time. But that did not happen. Instead, on July 26, 1965, the National Art Schools were inaugurated, officially declared finished in their various states of completion.

NOTES

1. David Bigelman, interview with the author (November 1997).
2. José Mosquera, interview with the author (September 1997).
3. Porro considered the cultural enlightenment of his charges very much his mission as Gilberto Seguí notes in this account: "Porro had the habit, sometimes a bit aggressive, of making us aware of our cultural deficiencies, which were many. In his cultural crusade, he conducted a relentless campaign to make us read books, see films, attend concerts and visit exhibits that he deemed necessary to our cultural formation." G. Seguí, "Les odeurs de la rue," *La Havane 1952–1961, Série Mémoires* 31 (May 1994): 36 (author's translation).
4. José Mosquera, interview with the author (September 1997).
5. For an account of a former art student, Ever Fonseca, see Documents, herein.
6. R. Gottardi, interview with the author (June 1992).
7. V. Garatti, "Antologia su 'Le scuole nazionale d'arte di Cubanacán,' 1961–63," *Architettura e istruzione a Cuba*, Fiorese, Giorgio, ed. (Milan, CLUP, 1980): 63.
8. Besides the architects from this gathering, the National Art Schools had also received other important cultural dignitaries from abroad. Graham Greene, Alberto Moravia, Dacia Maraini, Tony Richardson, Joris Ivens, Andrzej Wajda, Vittoriano Viganó, Roberto Matta, and others were among the luminaries who visited the schools.

School of Dramatic Arts
ABOVE: *aerial view of construction* (PAOLO GASPARINI)
BELOW: *Roberto Gottardi (second from right) and model makers with model of theater*
(UNKNOWN PHOTOGRAPHER)

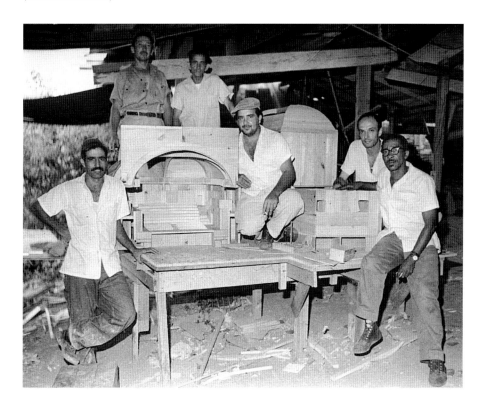

School of Music
ABOVE: *view of construction scaffolding, 1962* (MICHELENA)
BELOW: *concrete ring base for Catalan vaults, 1962* (MICHELENA)

School of Modern Dance
ABOVE: *aerial view of construction* (PAOLO GASPARINI)
BELOW: *carpenters erecting scaffold* (UNKNOWN PHOTOGRAPHER)

School of Ballet
ABOVE: *shower room enclosure at left, scaffolded dance pavilion at right, 1961* (MICHELENA)

OPPOSITE
TOP: *aerial view of construction* (PAOLO GASPARINI)
BOTTOM: *view toward performance pavilion under construction, 1962* (MICHELENA)

National Art Schools

School of Modern Dance
Ricardo Porro

The School of Modern Dance commands a ridge on the south side of the country club, overlooking the rest of the grounds. This assertive scheme draws cues from its prominent location. The program called for a performance theater, four dance class pavilions, classrooms, a library and administration facilities, which Porro assembled in a dynamic play of forms.

> I was in love with the Revolution and it was this emotional response that prompted a new direction in my architecture. Architecture must take into account the need to create a potent image compatible with the purpose of the building. This may incorporate references to tradition, to the problems of our time, or to the eternal problems of mankind. In other words a work of architecture must have *meaning*. Architecture must add a poetic dimension to everyday life.
>
> In the School of Modern Dance I wanted to express two very powerful sentiments produced by the first stage, the romantic stage, of the Revolution: the exaltation, collective emotional explosion, but at the same time a sense of anguish and fear confronting an unknown future. The entrance and the dance pavilions are the image of exaltation. The fragmented vaults above appear inflated by an expansive force. Upon passing through the portals that lead to the plaza the angles of the columns point in different directions, breaking the order and provoking disorientation, anguish. At the same time I tried to play with the dancer's sense of movement. When the dancer leaps, the surrounding space expands—explodes—around him. And this is what I tried to create in the interior of the dance pavilions. But at the same time the sensation of explosion was that of the emotional explosion that the country was living at that moment.[9]

Porro conceived the plan metaphorically as a sheet of glass that had been violently smashed by a fist and fragmented into shifting shards, symbolic of the Revolution's overthrow of the old order. The fragments gather

ABOVE: *Aerial view, 1965* (PAOLO GASPARINI)

OPPOSITE: *Plan* (ALEX BRITO AND WILLIAM DUNCANSON)

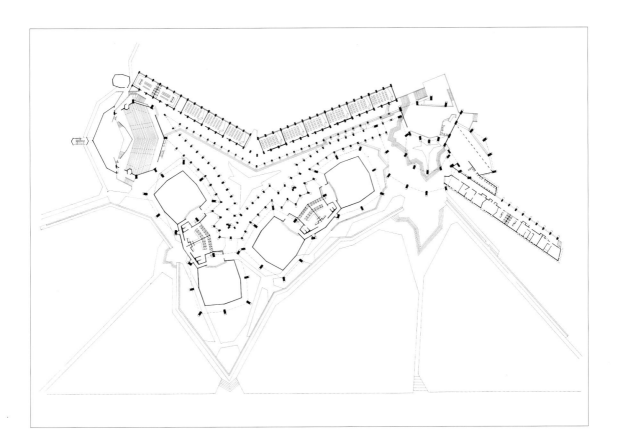

around an entry plaza—the locus of the "impact"—and develop into an urban scheme of linear, though non rectilinear, shifting streets and courtyards. Three Catalan vaults celebrate a triumphal entry. Others form the enclosures for the studios, classrooms and administration buildings, softening in volume what is angular in plan. The shifting geometries of the plan cause the exterior spaces and passageways to expand and contract in a dynamic construct, prefiguring the formal preoccupations of many architects today.

The entry arches form a hinge around which the library and administrative bar rotate away from the rest of the school. The south side of the fragmented plaza is defined by the rotating dance pavilions, paired around shared dressing rooms. The north edge, facing a sharp drop in terrain, is made by two linear bars containing classrooms, that form an obtuse angle. At the end of the angular procession, farthest from the entry, where the plaza once again compresses is the performance theater.

This was the first of the schools under construction. Ricardo Porro had prepared the plans in less than two months' time. For all practical purposes, the School of Modern Dance can be considered complete as originally envisioned, even though some interior work remained unfinished. The dance pavilions are particularly celebrated spaces. The unfolding of the interior of the cupola and the layered walls expanding outward

and upward, describe the expansion of space that Porro recognized in the movements of the dancer. The Catalan vault is used throughout in a variety of shapes covering a diverse set of plastic volumes. However, the engineers at the Ministry of Construction, not trusting the structural potential of the Catalan vault, imposed a conservative structure on the dance pavilions' domed enclosures. Nevertheless, Porro turned this to advantage, expressing the musculature of the reinforced concrete frame for the domes, incorporating it into planters, a gesture integrating landscape into the fabric of the building. Unlike the other schools which have exposed brickwork throughout, the walls, piers and other vertical elements in the Modern Dance School are sheathed in a thick rustic stucco, reminiscent of Le Corbusier's chapel at Ronchamp, setting off the Catalan vaults which remain exposed in natural terra cotta.

NOTES
1. R. Porro, interview with the author (July 1992).

OPPOSITE: *Dance pavilion, interior view, 1965* (PAOLO GASPARINI)
BELOW: *Cafeteria, interior view, 1965* (PAOLO GASPARINI)

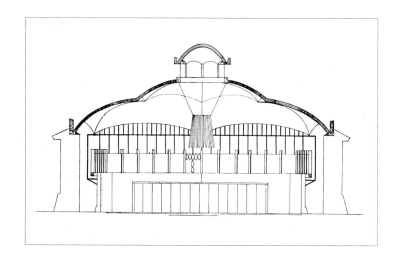

OPPOSITE
TOP: *Section through dance pavilion* (COURTESY RICARDO PORRO)
BOTTOM: *Cupolas with planters built into structural frame, 1965* (PAOLO GASPARINI)

ABOVE: *Landscaped view from exterior, 1965* (PAOLO GASPARINI)

ABOVE: *Entry courtyard, 1965* (PAOLO GASPARINI)

OPPOSITE
TOP: *View toward dance pavilion from main plaza, 1992* (JOHN A. LOOMIS)
BOTTOM: *Entry courtyard, 1992* (JOHN A. LOOMIS)

School of Modern Dance

ABOVE: *Vaulted entry, 1965* (PAOLO GASPARINI)
OPPOSITE: *Vaulted entry, 1992* (JOHN A. LOOMIS)

School of Modern Dance

School of Plastic Arts
Ricardo Porro

The School of Plastic Arts is located at the entrance to the former country club, on a flat grassy site across from the clubhouse at the northern perimeter of the site. It is the most visible and accessible of the five schools and therefore the one most often identified with the complex. Its vaulted walkways and domed studios seem to hover over the green meadow. The program consisted mostly of studios, ten in total, with exhibition space, offices and some classrooms. As in the School of Modern Dance, the forms of the School of Plastic Arts were determined through a spatialized symbolic representation. However, here the figurative iconography engaged issues of gender and culture that would prove controversial. Porro sought to address issues of identity through an architectural synthesis of Cuba's multicultural heritage, which he defined as a hybrid of patriarchal Spanish baroque culture and nurturing matriarchal African culture, both mediated by the sensuality of the tropics. The issues that Porro had first raised in his article "El sentido de la tradición," now developed into a formal imagery.

> The Revolution had been for me a cataclysm, and a very good one at that. I now wished to refute both architecture's and my own family's aristocratic past. I wanted to seek an expression of an architecture for the people and to delve into the eternal problems of the human condition. The School of Plastic Arts is the expression of beginnings—the beginning of my creative life and the beginning of the Revolution.

> In the moment that I conceived the School of Plastic Arts I was interested very much in the problem of tradition. Cuba is not Catholic. Cuba is a country where the African religion has more force than the Catholic. So I tried to make an *arquitectura negra*, a city seized by a *negritud* that had never before had a presence in architecture. While it had been given a presence in the paintings of Lam, to draw from Cuba's African culture in architecture was a radical step.[10]

OPPOSITE: *View between curved colonnades, 1965*
(PAOLO GASPARINI)

Cuba is sensual. Everything touches the senses and there is nothing strange about this. It is an island bathed by the breeze, with a smooth and gentle landscape that a hand can almost caress. . . . The fertile soil is sensual as is the walk of a Cuban woman. The Spanish austerity was lost in this sensuality. The whites profited from this sensuality and over time produced a more modified *barroco criollo*. . . . The mysticism and tragedy of the Spanish baroque never had validity in Cuba, they were left behind in the mother country. What came was a miniaturized, simplified and sweetened form.[11]

Sensuality and sexuality are noted everywhere. Among fruits, the papaya is the feminine sex. The open mamey with its perspiration and its color—what does it suggest? Pass the tongue over the mango seed and see how the palm tree penetrates the ground! . . . And a politician puffing on a big dark cigar, is that not sublime! . . .

So this calm and sensual Cuban baroque from the eighteenth and nineteenth centuries arrived in the twentieth century with an explosion, an apotheosis. I believe that this was a very correct evolution for Cuba. It exists in Lezama and in Sarduy. In Cuba this new baroque is fully expressed. It is also that which I wished to express in my School of Plastic Arts.[12]

Porro's poetically interpretive reading of Cuban history provided a theoretical framework for a formal elaboration of cultural themes heretofore unknown in Cuban architecture. The plan of the school evokes an archetypal African village, creating an organic urban complex of streets, buildings and open spaces. The studios, oval in plan, are the basic cell of the complex. Each one was conceived as a small arena theater with a central skylight to serve students working from a live model. The studios are organized along two arcs, two curving colonnaded paths. Lecture rooms and offices are accommodated in a contrasting blocklike plan that is partially wrapped by and engaged with the colonnaded path. The Catalan vaulted cupolas over the studio pavilions bear reference to both Borromini and the female breast. There was also a triple domed exhibition space with a central column where the vaults converged, and a contrasting rectangular block which housed classrooms and administration.

Porro's desire to create an architecture that was evocative of the female was in part a response to the poem *Eupalinos* by Paul Valéry, in which Eupalinos, an architect, decides to build a temple based on the proportions of a beautiful young girl he knows in Corinth. Ideas of gender and ethnicity converge in the curvilinear forms and spaces of the Plastic Arts School which are intended as evocations of *negritud* as well as of female nurturing and sensuality. For Porro sensuality was not just a condition of *negritud* or gender but also a condition of the generic erotic nature of the tropics that

ABOVE: *Aerial view, 1965* (PAOLO GASPARINI)
BELOW: *Plan* (ALEX BRITO)

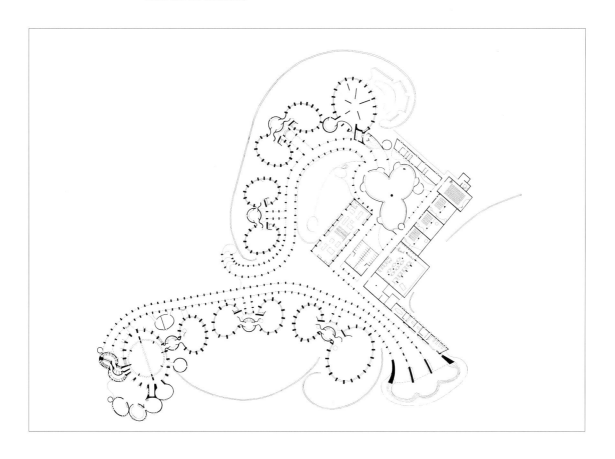

School of Plastic Arts

invited open expression of sexuality. He brought together these readings of the building with the phrase, "La Escuela de Artes Plásticas es la ciudad que se convierte en Eros."[13]

Three Catalan vaults leading to three diverging colonnaded paths present themselves at the entrance. The central path, however, ends unexpectedly, compelling one to choose one of the flanking paths. The curving paths deny the visual orientation common to linear perspectival organization. Following this *paseo arquitectónico* is a disorienting experience since one is never quite sure where one is. Arrival at the main plaza is indirect and comes as a surprise. Here one encounters Porro's most overt and literal reference to the body and sexuality, a fountain in the form of a papaya, a fruit with distinct sexual connotations in the Caribbean, filling a pool surrounded by limp phallus-like drains. Here at the culmination of the journey, the erotic is no longer suggestive, but representationally explicit. But beyond the erotic episodes, it is the organic spatial experience of Porro's choreographed *paseo arquitectónico* and the magic realist sensation of disorientation formed through plastic manipulation of Catalan vault that make this complex distinctive.

NOTES

1. Porro, interview with the author (July 1992)
2. R. Porro, "Cuba y Yo," *Escandalar—Cuba Otra* 17–18 (January/June 1982): 154.
3. Ibid., 155–6.
4. R. Porro, quoted in Patrice Goulet, *Ricardo Porro*, vol. 1 of *Partitions*, 2 vols., (Paris: Institut Français d'Architecture, 1993). (author's translation)

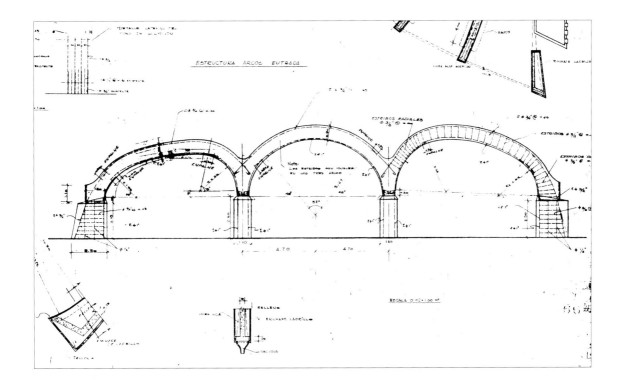

TOP: *Construction detail of vaulted entry* (COURTESY RICARDO PORRO)
BOTTOM: *View toward entry, 1965* (PAOLO GASPARINI)

School of Plastic Arts

ABOVE: *Roofscape, 1965* (PAOLO GASPARINI)
OPPOSITE: *Landscaped view from exterior, 1965* (PAOLO GASPARINI)

School of Plastic Arts

ABOVE: *Interior view of sculpture studio, 1965* (PAOLO GASPARINI)

OPPOSITE
TOP: *Section of through studio* (COURTESY RICARDO PORRO)
BOTTOM: *Painting studio, 1975* (JOSE ALBERTO FIGUEROA)

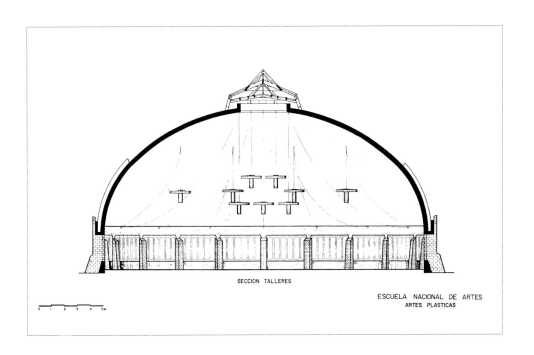

SECCION TALLERES

ESCUELA NACIONAL DE ARTES
ARTES PLASTICAS

0   1   2   3   4   5M

School of Plastic Arts   (65)

ABOVE: *Exhibition gallery, 1965*
(PAOLO GASPARINI)

RIGHT: *Exhibition gallery, 1975*
(JOSÉ ALBERTO FIGUEROA)

OPPOSITE
TOP: *Central entry vault, 1992*
(JOHN A. LOOMIS)

BOTTOM: *Colonnade, 1992*
(JOHN A. LOOMIS)

School of Plastic Arts

OPPOSITE: *Main plaza with fountain, 1965* (PAOLO GASPARINI)
ABOVE: *Main plaza with fountain, 1992* (JOHN A. LOOMIS)

School of Dramatic Arts
Roberto Gottardi

The School of Dramatic Arts lies to the east of the School of Modern Dance on a site that steps down to a densely vegetated bend in the Rio Quibú. This school and the School of Music would have been the largest of the complex, had they been built to their entirety. The original program for the School of Dramatic Arts was extensive, complicated, and without clear precedents. The school was to contain both a large indoor theater and a smaller amphitheater with a shared stage and technical support. Various types of classrooms, studios and administrative facilities made up the rest of the program, which also included a cafeteria and library. Instead of symbolic or cultural references, Gottardi's approach to the School of Dramatic Arts reflects an intimate relationship to program and process, and an interpretation of program as both subject and object of design.

Conceptually, the theater constituted a center of mass from which other functions, technical, pedagogical, support were organized. The more theoretical classes were located on the exterior, the more practical classes just inside, and at the center, experimentation within the theater itself. When it was time for a performance, everything would come together. The attention toward the theater was accentuated by the roofs which were inflected inward toward the theater. The school was organized like a small community bearing in mind the character of a theater company. Theater is made with actors, directors, sound technicians, set designers, costume designers, etc. It is important to see all these members as part of the community. The streets are the means to both bring together all the disciplines and to provide informal places for the individuals of the community to meet and sit. Inside the complex there is a sense of being in an environment completely apart from the outside, like the hermetically social experience of being part of a theater company. The circular form facilitates a certain independence. It provides a special experience that could not derive from a linear form. The spaces follow in an unanticipated manner. Also, many spaces that are not theater, can be used as theater. In a certain

OPPOSITE: *Courtyard amphitheater, 1992*
(JOHN A. LOOMIS)

sense, all parts of the school can be used as a theater. The theater is a school and the school is a theater, like Antonin Artaud's concept of the "theater and its double."[1]

The complex was originally intended to be comprised of three units, each organized around open courts and connected to each other by the landscaped terraces stepping down to meet the river. The administrative, library, and cafeteria facilities were partially built and abandoned. The unit housing classrooms around the double patios was never built, nor was the flanking storage facility. Likewise, the aforementioned theater, part of the primary complex, was never constructed, except for a few pylons, leaving open one side of what should have been a closed system. The unbuilt theater would have functioned in three ways: opening to an enclosed audience as a typical proscenium theater, opening to an exterior courtyard audience, or opening to an audience surrounding the performance on all sides. What was constructed was the tightly knit complex of classrooms surrounding the courtyard amphitheater. As built, Gottardi's school, which integrates the experience of learning and performing, and embodies the essence of collectivity, holds together remarkably well due to the strength and integrity of its scheme.

Like Porro's two schools, the Dramatic Arts School is urban in concept. It is organized as a very compact, axial, cellular plan around the central courtyard amphitheater. The amphitheater, fronting the unbuilt theater, at what now is the entrance, is the focal point of all the subsidiary functions, which are grouped around it. The narrow leftover interstices, open to the sky like streets, serve as circulation routes between the positive volumes of the masonry cells. This is quite the opposite of the other schools where the *paseo arquitectónico* is celebrated instead through the positive connective tissue of its elongated vaulted passageways. Winding more or less concentrically through the complex, the circulation experientially negates the axiality and generalized symmetry that organize the plan. This presents an interesting formal contradiction. While quite ordered in plan, the experience of walking through the streets seems random and spontaneous. This school turns its back to the landscape and looks inward to an interiorized environment that is evocative of a north African or Mediterranean urban vernacular. And like true vernacular, the harmony of its forms and materials in a unified organic construct, provide an architectural continuity despite the missing elements.

NOTES
1. R. Gottardi, interview with the author (June 1992).

TOP: *Model* (DAVID BIGELMAN, PHOTOGRAPH: ALBERTO KORDA)
BOTTOM: *Plan* (ALEX BRITO AND WILLIAM DUNCANSON)

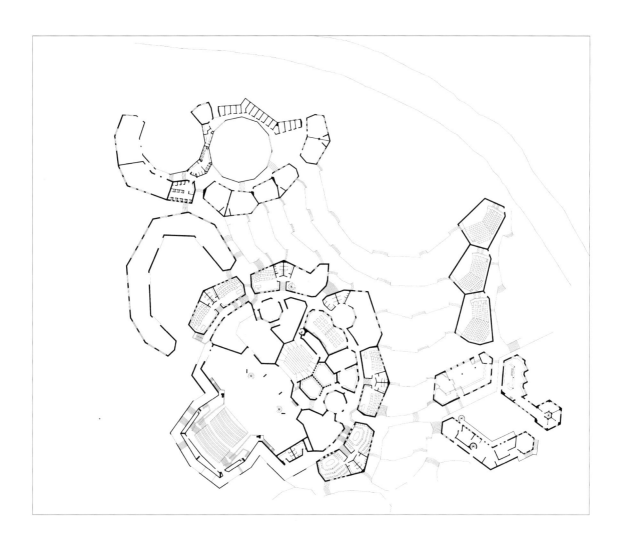

School of Dramatic Arts

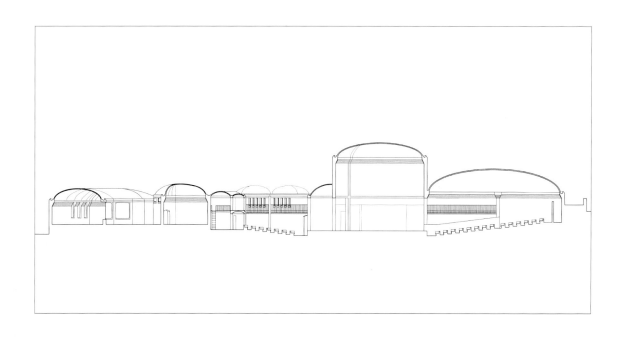

OPPOSITE
TOP: *Longitudinal section through complex and unbuilt theater* (WILLIAM DUNCANSON)
BOTTOM: *View of passage, 1992* (JOHN A. LOOMIS)

ABOVE: *Courtyard amphitheater, 1997* (HAZEL HANKIN)

Interior streetscapes
ABOVE AND AT RIGHT: *(HAZEL HANKIN, 1994)*
OPPOSITE: *(JOHN A. LOOMIS, 1992)*

School of Dramatic Arts

ABOVE: *Performance space, 1997* (HAZEL HANKIN)

OPPOSITE
TOP: *Interior streetscape, 1997* (JOSÉ ALBERTO FIGUEROA)
BOTTOM: *Exterior view of classroom, 1997* (JOHN A. LOOMIS)

School of Dramatic Arts

OPPOSITE: *Detail of built-in classroom seating, 1992* (JOHN A. LOOMIS)

ABOVE
TOP: *Classroom, 1997* (JOSÉ ALBERTO FIGUEROA)
BOTTOM: *Performance classroom, 1997* (JOSÉ ALBERTO FIGUEROA)

ABOVE: *Abandoned construction, 1997* (JOSÉ ALBERTO FIGUEROA)

OPPOSITE
TOP: *Pylons for unbuilt theater, 1992* (JOHN A. LOOMIS)
BOTTOM: *Abandoned construction, 1997* (JOHN A. LOOMIS)

School of Dramatic Arts   (83)

School of Music
Vittorio Garatti

The School of Music by Vittorio Garatti embraces a hillside roughly paralleling the river. The school provides classroom facilities, individual practice rooms, and group rehearsal and lecture rooms. In addition to these pedagogical facilities, the complex was intended to include a symphonic concert hall, an opera, hall and administrative services, which remain unbuilt. The scheme was formed primarily out of a response to the site.

Primary among our design principles was the intention for the architecture to be integral with the landscape. I selected two sites where the character of the terrain would have to inform the design. There are several vectors of analysis that lead to design. First is the analysis of the landscape and the physical context. There is also the analysis of function which is very decisive in plan organization. Then one must consider cultural vectors; Wifredo Lam for example was for me an important inspiration. And there are vectors having to do with history, precedent, typology. These were the kinds of things [Ernesto] Rogers made us very much aware of. Some of these vectors are internal forces and some are external in the way they influence the design process. The architect has to work back and forth among these different sets of information, usually with great difficulty, especially in the beginning, to generate a design. Eventually the process becomes self-generating. The work begins to transcend the data and becomes something unto itself in which none of the original pieces of information is any longer recognizable. The creative process when it becomes truly self-generating, as [Jean-François] Lyotard says, can result in something that is unrecognizable, illegible to the artist himself. So the artist has to have a certain amount of faith in what emerges from the process.

I have always thought of a design project like a trip, and the attention one has to pay in packing one's suitcase. In my suitcase there are the records of Johann Sebastian Bach, of Igor Stravinski, of Béla Bartók, the paintings of Lam (introduced to me by Porro) the books of Lezama Lima and Alejo Carpentier, and naturally "The Revolution" which was the spark to my creative process.[1]

OPPOSITE: *Recital hall, 1997*
(JOHN A. LOOMIS)

The School of Music is constructed as a serpentine ribbon 330 meters long, traversing the contours of the landscape and almost touching the river at both its "head" and "tail." Adjacent to the central body of the ribbon was to have been a piazza around which the concert hall, opera hall, library and administration would have been constructed. The serpentine scheme and its *paseo arquitectónico* begins with the "tail" where a group of curved brick planters step up from the river, initiating the sequence. At first the curvilinear band contains individual practice rooms and the exterior colonade. This passage then submerges as the band is joined by another layer containing larger group practice rooms and another exterior colonade, shifted up in section from the original band. The idea was to facilitate easy movement between individual practice and group practice. There is also a series of other upward displacements that occur along the procession. These displacements are read in the roofs as a series of terrace-like planters for flowers. Garatti likens the development of the classrooms, which follow the terracing, to the Bath Crescent. Transversally, this 15-meter-wide "tube," broken into two levels is covered by undulating Catalan vaults. These layered vaults emerge organically from the landscape, traversing the contours of the ground plane. Garatti's meandering *paseo arquitectónico* presents an ever changing contrast of light and shadow, of dark subterranean and brilliant tropical environments. The functional organization along the path continues to proceed programmatically in scale from smaller to larger uses, culminating in a concert hall that wraps around an ancient and monumental jagüey tree from whose branches drape huge roots. The constructed landscape again steps downward with a series of curved brick planters that return to the river.

NOTES

1. V. Garatti, interview with the author (November 1997).

CAPTIONS OPPOSITE
TOP: *Plan* (ALEX BRITO AND WILLIAM DUNCANSON)
CENTER: *Model, 1962* (MICHELENA)
BOTTOM: *Aerial view, 1965* (VITTORIO GARATTI)

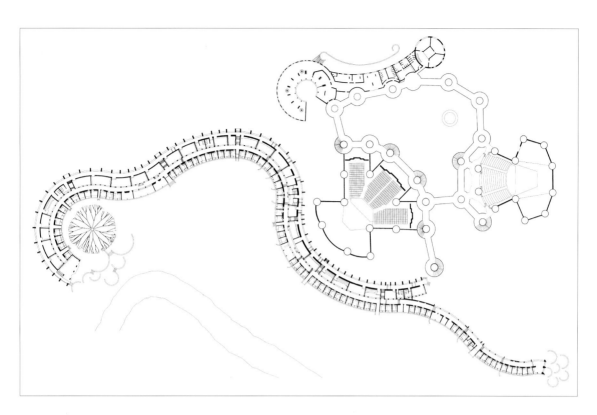

School of Music

ABOVE: *Roofscape, 1963* (MAYITO)

OPPOSITE
TOP: *Exterior view, 1992* (JOHN A. LOOMIS)
BOTTOM: *Roofscape, 1992* (JOHN A. LOOMIS)

School of Music

OPPOSITE: *Covered passage, 1992*
(JOHN A. LOOMIS)

LEFT: *Balcony and entry to recital hall, 1992* (JOHN A. LOOMIS)

BELOW: *Subterranean corridor, 1965*
(MICHELENA)

School of Music

ABOVE: *Model of concert hall, 1962* (MICHELENA)

OPPOSITE
TOP: *Abandoned classroom, 1992* (JOHN A. LOOMIS)
BOTTOM: *Occupied classroom, 1992* (JOHN A. LOOMIS)

School of Music

ABOVE: *Recital hall, 1992* (JOHN A. LOOMIS)

OPPOSITE
TOP: *Detail at exterior of recital hall, 1997* (JOHN A. LOOMIS)
CENTER: *View to recital hall from balcony, 1992* (JOHN A. LOOMIS)
BOTTOM: *Planters at beginning of* paseo arquitectónico, *1992* (JOHN A. LOOMIS)

School of Music

School of Ballet

Vittorio Garatti

The School of Ballet lies just south of the School of Music, across the Rio Quibú, nestled into a lushly vegetated ravine at its bend. The program was somewhat similar to that of the School of Modern Dance, calling for a large performance theater, three dance class pavilions, classrooms, a library and administration facilities. But for Vittorio Garatti, the site called for a radically different and equally original scheme.

Our design freedom was total, even in the choice of site. For the School of Ballet, we found a small valley from which the approach was from above. That would have permitted me to have almost hidden it. At first I thought of burying the School of Ballet, but that proved too expensive. Ironically, today, with the help of nature, the building has spontaneously become submerged. The first sensation looking at the terrain was to descend toward the opening below, describing an "S" with open arms like a child playing airplane. This "S" became the spine of the structure for the design. The choice of the pavilion type was a common one between Porro and myself. We both attended practice sessions of the dancers and we observed that while they were dancing, they were designing space. But they were psychologically crushed by the walls and the ceiling. Therefore we chose to construct cupolas and curved lateral walls, (in my case convex) that could collect the movements of the dancers. This movement was perhaps one of the principle characteristics. There was also a preoccupation on my part concerning representation. I wanted the school to be extremely dynamic, in part as a response to the dynamism of dance. But I wanted the school to be dynamic, not only because it was a ballet school, but because it was to be a vision of our future. Dynamic, at the same time expressing freedom, open in all directions where you could come and go as you wished. Therefore, there was also to be a freedom of use for all parts of the building, even the roof. I imagined that in the evening the students would gather up there and stroll, study, exercise or dance as the sun set. The School of Ballet was to be something which could be used, experienced throughout.[1]

From the top of a ravine one looks down upon the complex, nestled into the descending gorge. The plan of the School of Ballet is articulated by a cluster of domed volumes, connected by an organic layering of Catalan vaults that follow the serpentine path. There are at least five ways to enter the complex. The most dramatic starts at the top of the ravine with a simple path bisected by a notch to carry rainwater. As one proceeds, the terra-cotta cupolas, articulating the major programmatic spaces, emerge floating over the lush growth. The path then descends downward into the serpentine passage that links the three dance pavilions, administration pavilions, grand performance space, and library. A partially subterranean arc extending toward the river contains classrooms. The path leads not only into the complex, but also up onto its roofs which are an integral part of Garatti's *paseo arquitectónico*. The essence of the design is not to be found so much in the plan but in the spatial experience of the school's choreographed volumes that move with the descending ravine.

In creating this dynamic spatial experience, Garatti pushed the structural potential of the Catalan vault farther than any of the other projects. In none of the other schools are they as thin or as audacious in the apparent act of defying gravity. The spans of the dance pavilions are a clear 17 meters, and the dome of the large performance hall covers a diameter of 34 meters. The vaults were also elements used to modulate and choreograph light. In the organic interior pathways, the Catalan vaults peel away allowing slices of the brilliant tropical light to penetrate the dark subterranean corridor. Likewise, there is a dramatic contrast upon leaving the dark pathway and entering the brightly lit volumes of the dance pavilions. Here the light was modulated differently employing an element from Cuba's *arquitectura criolla* that Garatti had witnessed in Trinidad, *medio puntos*, wooden louvers fanning out in a half circle, in the arches of the cupolas. And there are other examples of the dramatic effects of light from the central oculus in the dome of the performance hall to the clerestories over the showers and toilets in the changing rooms.

Garatti also refers to this as an architecture of the garden, with roots in various Mediterranean traditions—Moorish, Spanish and Sicilian. In this spirit, he appropriated the element of water and combined it with the wall to create another kind of celebration of circulation and path. Notched with a channel for water, the garden walls descend from the roof, wind their way through the school's volumes and onto the grounds, providing the constant pleasure of the sound and sight of water returning and merging into the landscape. But that is not all that merges into the landscape, for today the School of Ballet lies completely abandonded and in ruins, engulfed by the jungle in the lush ravine.

NOTES
1. V. Garatti, interview with the author (July 1992).

TOP: *Elevation* (WILLIAM DUNCANSON)
BOTTOM: *Roofscape, 1965* (PAOLO GASPARINI)

School of Ballet

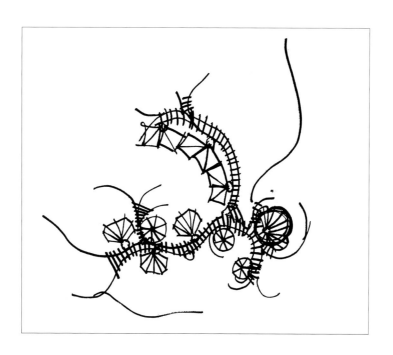

TOP: *Sketch, 1961* (VITTORIO GARATTI)
BOTTOM: *Vittorio Garatti and Alberto Moravia, 1970* (UNKNOWN PHOTOGRAPHER)

OPPOSITE
TOP: *Plan* (ALEX BRITO AND WILLIAM DUNCANSON)
BOTTOM: *Aerial view* (PAOLO GASPARINI)

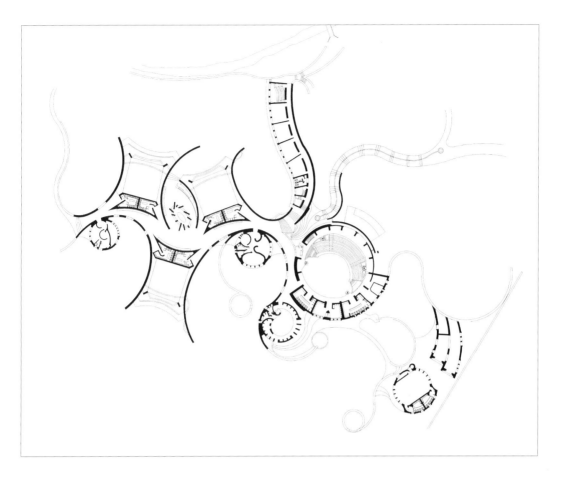

School of Ballet

ABOVE: *Entry, 1965* (PAOLO GASPARINI)
RIGHT: *Foyer, 1963* (VITTORIO GARATTI)

OPPOSITE
TOP: *Roofscape of elliptical courtyard, 1965* (PAOLO GASPARINI)
BOTTOM: *View into elliptical courtyard, 1963* (UNKNOWN PHOTOGRAPHER)

School of Ballet

ABOVE: *Roofscape, 1965* (PAOLO GASPARINI)

OPPOSITE
TOP: *Roofscape, 1992* (JOHN A. LOOMIS)
BOTTOM: *Roofscape, 1997* (JOHN A. LOOMIS)

School of Ballet

OPPOSITE
TOP: *Entry, 1992* (JOHN A. LOOMIS)
BOTTOM: *Foyer, 1997* (JOHN A. LOOMIS)

ABOVE: *Dance pavilion, 1997* (JOHN A. LOOMIS)

School of Ballet

OPPOSITE
TOP: *Library, 1994* (HAZEL HANKIN)
LEFT: *Administration, 1997* (JOHN A. LOOMIS)
RIGHT: *Shower room, 1997* (JOHN A. LOOMIS)

ABOVE: *Performance pavilion, 1997* (JOHN A. LOOMIS)

School of Ballet

Aunque sepas que no, dile que sí

Si lo contradices, peor para ti.

"Canción para mi abuelo Paco"

Pedro Luis Ferrer

Crime and Punishment

The National Art Schools had been conceived in 1961 during a period of optimism and enthusiasm, but by 1965 it was clear that something had gone terribly wrong. Their subsequent neglect and abandonment were not merely the result of redirected national priorities necessitated by economic concerns. In the increasingly doctrinaire political environment, the schools became subject to a series of ideologically framed attacks that resulted in their repudiation. Their ostracism would bear unfortunate consequences for the future of architecture in revolutionary Cuba.

The repudiation of the National Art Schools took place in an evolving political and cultural context that is worth examining. Cuba, having been humiliated for years by the Platt amendment, was at the time of the Revolution still very much subject to U.S. political and economic control. The new revolutionary leadership, not yet fully radicalized, nevertheless had also inherited profound anti-imperialist (anti-U.S.) sentiments that had their roots in the nineteenth century, and which had been strengthened by the four-year U.S. occupation after the War for Independence. The more recent demise of Guatemala's democratically elected reformist government in 1954, at the hands of the CIA, left no illusions as to North American tolerance of true independence. After Cuba's embrace of Marxism-Leninism, in 1961, economic and social reforms would in time come to take on the contours of one-party rule, central planning, and state control of the means of production. By that time, the KGB had already upgraded their formerly skeptical code name for Cuba from *Yountsie* (Youngsters) to the more optimistic *Avanpost* (Bridgehead), and a growing emulation of the Soviet model would ensue.

Nonetheless, it is also true that in practice, and in the eyes of many Latin Americans and Cubans, at the outset, the island revolution represented a major break with the Soviet model. It was freer, more democratic, disorderly, tropical, and spontaneous, as well as being intellectually more diverse and politically more liberal. With time the resemblance between the models would grow, and Cuba would come to look much more like the Soviet Union. But in the early stages, at least, the discontinuities clearly outweighed the similarities.[1]

With time, through its reforms, Cuba would eliminate the severest forms of poverty so common throughout Latin America and the developing world. Cuba's revolution would also provide a basic level of education and health care for most of its population, remarkable achievements for a small, underdeveloped, isolated country. But these achievements would come at a significant price—a dependency upon the Soviet Union that affected many aspects of peoples' lives. Lisandro Otero, Cuban writer and former cultural attaché to the Soviet Union, summed up this phenomenon retrospectively in a 1991 interview: "In the Revolution there was a whole aspect of freshness, spontaneity, and originality that faded as we began to adopt more and more Soviet patterns of behavior, from the red kerchiefs to centralized planning. . . ."[2]

The National Art Schools were indeed a product of the original "freshness, spontaneity, and originality" that would inevitably come to conflict with the changing political culture. The initial opposition that the schools encountered was technical, however, not ideological. Most of the engineers in the Ministry of Construction distrusted the Catalan vault and were strongly opposed to its employment. Ricardo Porro recalls:

> I was called to the Ministry to a meeting with all the engineers. They told me that the Catalan vault was an absurdity and that I did not know what I was doing. The schools were going to fall down and kill the children of workers. How could I be so arrogant! It was a great struggle to realize the Catalan vaults.[3]

But the use of the Catalan vault was approved after Gumersindo had successfully constructed a prototype which he tested under loads, and after structural engineer Hilda Fernández had produced supportive structural calculations. Nevertheless, skeptical engineers imposed on certain spans the employment of steel tension rods—utterly superfluous elements given the lack of lateral thrust inherent in the Catalan vault. But in the beginning, criticism was mostly just an irritation, because the schools had the support of the most important person of all, Fidel Castro. In time this would change.

Even though the Catalan vault had been approved and work was advancing, opposition to the structural system continued, coming mostly from mid-level functionaries, both engineers and architects, at MICONS. This opposition often masked a much more subjective agenda, fueled

Construction of the vaults at the School of Music, 1962 (MICHELENA)

by a petty combination of fear and envy, that only later assumed an
ideological dimension. The plastic forms emerging from the landscape in
Cubanacán were a refutation of the rationalist principles upon which
modern architecture and the professional formation of these newly
appointed bureaucrats rested. The late Antonio Quintana, an accomplished architect before the Revolution, held strong mainstream modernist
convictions, and was a central figure in the jockeying for power within
the bureaucracy of the newly formed MICONS. He felt particularly threatened by the "organic" heresy occurring in Cubanacán. Vehement in his
opposition, he formed a nucleus for other detractors. There was also
resentment of the comparatively privileged and unproletarian environment in which the art schools' team worked, the luxurious country club
with its still well-maintained facilities. Moreover, the schools' architects
answered directly to the minister, bypassing the intermediate layers of
bureaucrats who felt slighted.

Many of the young members of the design team were, like Porro himself, former members of the bourgeoisie and not of proletarian extraction.
Some critics questioned Ricardo Porro's revolutionary credentials because
he had been in exile during the armed struggle from 1958 on, even though
he had declared himself a Marxist long before many others. (Exile, it is
worth noting, did not hinder the careers of other cultural figures such as
Wifredo Lam, Alicia Alonso, Roberto Retamar, and Alejo Carpentier.) And
of course Roberto Gottardi and Vittorio Garatti were Italian, not Cuban,
and easily considered outsiders in a country with strong nationalist sensi-
bilities, even though "internationalism" was now the order of the day. All
of these factors, no doubt, contributed to the smoldering antagonism
within the Ministry of Construction. The minister, Osmany Cienfuegos,
remained cautiously detached as the controversy escalated.

Another contributing factor to the repudiation of the schools was the fact that building construction in Cuba was becoming increasingly influenced by the adoption of Soviet models. The Soviet Union and Eastern European countries had responded to their serious need for massive postwar reconstruction by developing standardized building types that initially followed the prewar neoclassical dictates of Stalin's social realism. With Stalin's death, however, and the rise of Nikita Khrushchev in 1953, the aesthetics of social realism in architecture were inverted. Moreover, because of Khrushchev's concern for efficiency in the economics of construction, standardization was extended beyond type and into the production of building components, such that by 1958 70% of these were prefabricated, significantly up from 25% in 1950. However, this technological orientation, instead of introducing flexibility and multiple options into building systems, resulted in a formal and typological rigidity. Soviet architecture's adoption of the most simplistic functionalist tendencies of the Modern Movement led to an anonymous and reductive aesthetic of the frame and the panel. For the Soviet architect, the result was a further suppression of individual creativity and the devaluing of the profession's role in design. Priorities were clearly delineated by Nikita Khrushchev in 1954 in a speech to the All Union Conference of Builders and Architects, titled "Remove Shortcomings in Design, Improve Work of Architects":

Comrades! Successful industrialization, improvement in the quality and reduction in the cost of building depend to a considerable extent on design organizations, on the work of architects and designers.

The interests of industrializing construction dictate the need to reorganize the work of design organizations and to make standardized designing and application of existing standardized designs the chief thing in their work. Widespread use of reinforced-concrete parts, sections, large blocks and new and effective materials is a new element in building techniques which imperatively requires us to give up obsolete design methods. (Applause)

[W]e have tolerated shortcomings in training architects. Many young architects who have scarcely crossed the threshold of the institute and have not yet got properly on their feet follow the example of masters of architecture and wish to design only buildings of an individual character, are in a hurry to build monuments to themselves. While Pushkin created for himself a monument unwrought by human hands, many architects want to create for themselves monuments 'wrought by human hands' in the form of buildings built according to individualized designs. (Laughter, applause)

To introduce standardized designs we must be determined and persistent, for we may meet resistance in this matter. Evidently there are some people who need a good explanation of the necessity for standardized designs.

The use of standardized designs in building will have a tremendous effect on economizing, speeding up and improving construction work. Of this there is no doubt. (Stormy applause)[4]

In Cuba, all sectors of design and construction, including the architecture school at the University of Havana, slowly succumbed to the Soviet model and progressively came under the centralized influence of MICONS. By November 1963 private architectural practice in Cuba had been abolished, and the professional association, the Colegio de Arquitectos, ceased to exist, its functions now absorbed into the Centro Técnico Superior de la Construcción. The architecture school became a subdepartment of the school of construction, which was under the administration of the Ministry of Construction. Most architects now became regarded as technicians, part of a team of engineers, who would resolve Cuba's many building needs through massive industrialized solutions that too often ignored the specifics of site and context, not to mention aesthetics.

Against this rapidly developing centralized framework for the production of architecture, the National Art Schools came to be seen as out of step and ideologically incorrect. According to Cuba's leading architectural historian, Roberto Segre,

> In [the schools] there was present an idealist ideology that still was conserving the attributes of an autonomous [capitalist] superstructure, elaborated by an intellectual elite, without direct contact with the base conditions and the social transformation carried forward by the revolutionary process.[5]

Much of what constituted the prosecutorial drama surrounding the schools went unrecorded. What can be regarded as the "official" critique is best documented in Segre's texts, which are representative of the types of criticism endured by the schools and their architects. Though this first account was published in 1968, three years after the inauguration of the schools, its ideological construct reflects much of the prior discourse that led to their repudiation.[6]

Segre's first text, *La Arquitectura de la Revolución Cubana* (see excerpt in Documents), faults the architects for not working together as a team and for their "individualism" in seeking a unique solution for each school. Furthermore, the article alleged that this individualism led to a "monumentalism," a condition that could only be associated with "authoritarianism," not in character with the Cuban Revolution, where authority is derived from the "people." The use and "glorification" of traditional materials and forms which look backward into history instead of forward into the revolutionary process were likewise questioned and rejected as not "scientific." The aesthetics of the schools were also criticized as representative of the static personal cultural gestures of the individual architects rather than the dynamic experience of a new society in transformation.

An expanded analysis appeared the following year in two books , *Diez Años de Arquitectura Revolucionaria en Cuba* and in *Cuba—Arquitectura de la Revolución*, also both by Segre. This analysis further defined the "errors" of the schools that caused them to fail to achieve a true revolutionary, socialist architectural identity. It then attempted to establish the correct values for this identity. In categorizing these errors as both programmatic and ideological, the critique faulted the architects for decisions that were outside their control. They were blamed for the remote location of the schools, though this had been a decision of Fidel Castro and Che Guevara. The architects were also blamed for not having designed an "efficient," "unified" complex with shared facilities, though separate facilities had been a decision of the board of directors of the art schools, who rejected the architects' original proposal of a single complex. There were also criticisms concerning function, though these were rarely specified in the texts. Some of these criticism may have had basis, such as the acoustical problems in some of the oval domed pavilions in the School of Plastic Arts, though Porro insists that had the acoustical baffles been installed as designed, this problem would have been solved. In Segre's summary of the situation,

> The real problems of the debate were about the rational use of resources, the standardization of constructive elements, the transformation of the social life of the working classes and the elaboration of a design methodology that permits itself to obtain the typological diversification in accordance with the new themes demanded by society.

> Therefore, the debate about artistic expression in the new revolutionary architecture was characterized by a fear of confronting industrialization and prefabrication. The value given to craft techniques, the persistence of the autonomy of design, the celebration of hypothetical Afro-Cuban roots, transformed the National Art Schools (which manifested a "cultured" orientation, aesthetically and formally) by a team of designers lead by Ricardo Porro, into an isolated, autonomous experience. . . . In other words, there existed an antagonism between a "privileged" work in the aesthetic and symbolic sense, and "standardized" construction, regarded in the pejorative sense according to a prejudice inherited from the architectonic production of the capitalist system.[7]

Critics of the art schools faulted the Catalan vault and masonry construction as constructive techniques that did not allow for transformable structures that could adapt to evolving needs. This criteria also had a symbolic component, as flexible building systems were associated with an unfolding socialist future, whereas fixed masonry structures signified a static capitalist past. Standardization and industrialization of construction, while ostensibly a pragmatic policy, was also one bound up in its own set of symbols that contained a "scientific" iconography expressive of a revolutionary socialist identity, more in tune with generalized universalist values than with those of culturally or ethnically specific identity. Of course, it had been conveniently forgotten by critics that the decision to use brick and tile had been an official one, made with the input and approval of MICONS itself, and the schools were well under construction by the time the first industrialized building system (the *Gran Panel* which was highly inflexible) from the USSR was introduced in 1963.[8]

Furthermore, this newly developed aversion in Cuba to the use of traditional brick and masonry construction techniques also reflected a Soviet prejudice. There is an illustrative anecdote from 1959 that comes from the construction of Akademgorodok, a new city in Siberia dedicated to scientific research. With the construction of the city already in progress for a year, all came to an abrupt halt when Khrushchev, upon learning that the buildings were being constructed of brick, called for the immediate change to prefabricated concrete panels. This actually slowed construction because the new factory that was to provide the building components could only meet one fifth of the demand. So massive prefabricated panels were inefficiently trucked in from hundreds of miles away and retrofitted into a design that had anticipated masonry construction. For Khrushchev, it seems brick was not only a technically "backward" material, but one representing bourgeois taste, which had no place in socialist architecture.

In addition to these objections to the architects' use of traditional building methods, the ideological errors the architects were alleged to have committed were categorized in the triumphalist rhetoric of the times: "individualism," "monumentalism," "historicism," "utopianism," "formalism," "grandiloquence," and driven by "aesthetic" criteria rather than "socialist rigor." The project was now considered "out of scale" with Cuba's needs and economic situation. The architects were described as "elitists" and "cultural aristocrats," whose work exhibited their "narcissistic" and "bourgeois" formation. Gottardi and Garatti, it was further charged "could not liberate themselves from Italian heritage, its medieval legacy, craft traditions and Neo-liberty [influence],"[9] charges which certainly did not reflect an "internationalist" position. Criticism consistently placed artistic expression and scientific process as opposing values.

Here it is interesting to examine some analogous situations that emerged in the early years of the Soviet Union after the Russian Revolution. The first years of Soviet power were also characterized by dynamic and diverse cultural manifestations in all the arts, especially in architecture. The situation in Russia was somewhat inverted, though. The Soviet avant garde held that all representations of the past must be eradicated, as they embodied the values of a decadent society. These architects sought to create completely new forms of expression, and created a large, diverse body of work that falls under the label "Constructivism," though it was produced by different, and often contentious, groups. The alternative view held that proletarian culture could selectively incorporate forms from the past if they were infused with new and progressive content. This latter view prevailed, and it led to a revival of classicism under Stalin, in contrast to Cuba which reflected Khrushchev's preference for a representation of functionalism. Architecture in both the Soviet Union and in Cuba was affected by power struggles that led to the centralization of the means of architectural production in *Arkhplan* in the Soviet Union by 1934 and in MICONS in Cuba by 1965. The subsequent repression of the Soviet avant garde, which was accused of "bourgeois formalism" and "utopianism," provided the political language that later would be used against the National Art Schools.

In understanding the drama that consumed the National Art Schools, it is helpful to consider the international context as well as the specific context of Cuba in the early 1960s. Part of the critique of the schools mirrored the "process versus form" debate that was occurring often in very politicized terms in Europe and North America. The issue of collective work versus individual creativity, expressed in Marxist terms, can be considered in part as a rearticulation of Walter Gropius's position that architecture should be the product of teamwork, not of individual talent. This position was disparagingly described by Aldo van Eyck as "dear industry, happy future, teamwork, no art, no prima donnas, kind of gruel."[10]

The criticism of traditional building methods must be seen also in terms of the larger argument for industrialized systems taking place internationally. While this tendency was dominant in the Soviet Union and the Eastern Bloc countries, it also had strong supporters in the West. Some architecture schools such as the Hochschule für Gestaltung at Ulm, under the influence of Tomás Maldonado, favored technology-driven programs, informed by social and economic issues that ultimately promoted industrialized building. It was during these same years that Moshe Safdie won the competition for the Montreal Habitat '67 with his prefabricated system. At the VIIth UIA Congress held in Havana in September 1963, where the low-tech art schools received an enthusiastic reception, the subject of

Humberto Alonso, Ciudad Universitaria José Antonio Echeverría (CUJAE), 1964
LEFT: *Block of classrooms;* RIGHT: *Courtyard between classroom blocks* (JOHN A. LOOMIS)

industrialized forms of construction was primary on the agenda. However, during this same period in both the Third and First Worlds, there were other architects besides Porro, Gottardi, and Garatti who instead of favoring industrialized systems, looked to low-tech means to resolve building needs. Nevertheless, with Cuba's growing alignment with the Soviet Union, it was not surprising that industrialized building systems, with their optimistic promises of efficiency, quality and quantity, would in a short time come to dominate Cuba's building policy. Again, it must be born in mind that the National Art Schools were first conceived and for the most part constructed before any such system appeared upon the island and before a truly intimate relationship with the USSR had developed.

On a related issue, the accusation that the schools were "historicist" presents an interesting parallel to Reyner Banham's 1959 attack on Ernesto Rogers for his "retreat from modern architecture." Nevertheless, the clash of passionate, and at times angry, positions in Europe and North America over all these issues resulted in a diversity of architectural production, whereas the one-sided discourse in Cuba eliminated diversity and left the country with a hegemonic approach to building.

The project that is universally used in Cuba as an example of the "correct" values of socialist architecture is the Ciudad Universitaria José Antonio Echeverría (CUJAE, 1964), a polytechnical university which became the new home for the architecture school, formerly part of the University of Havana located in El Vedado. The CUJAE was designed by the architect Humberto Alonso, formerly of Arquitectos Unidos, and it represents an alternative ideological position to that of the art schools. Located at a site

La Papaya, School of Plastic Arts, 1965
(PAOLO GASPARINI)

more remote from central Havana than Cubanacán, this project utilized lift-slab construction of prefabricated parts. Within this standardized constructive system, a successful relationship of solids and voids, spatial continuities and transparencies emerged, that are otherwise absent from much of Cuba's other examples of industrialized construction. It was a unique example, not to be repeated. Alonso left the country in September 1961 and the CUJAE's construction was completed by others, who then received credit for its design.

Perhaps as important as the criticism of the schools' use of traditional building methods and materials, was the disapproval of the references to Africa and the expressive sensuality in Porro's School of Plastic Arts. Although Afro-Cuban imagery richly inhabits the paintings of Wifredo Lam and Manuel Mendive, the sculpture of Agustín Cárdenas, the poetry of Nicolás Guillén and Alejo Carpentier, and many other artists very much celebrated by the Cuban Revolution, its appearance in architecture was criticized as "folkloric." Having origins in the historical tension between the *negrista* and Creole views on Cuban culture, the opposition toward

African imagery also reflected the contradictory cultural and political policy of the Cuban Revolution toward Afro-Cubans. The Cuban Revolution did indeed do much legislatively to end discrimination and improve the lot of the poor, the majority of whom were Afro-Cubans, estimated as being as much as 65% of the total population. Moreover, apart from the comparatively privileged *apparat*, Cuban society was becoming decisively more egalitarian. Structural vestiges of racism, however, persisted within the new institutions whose leadership was, and still is, predominantly white. Moreover, the Revolution's vision of *cubanidad* often seemed to be rooted more in the Creole tradition which regarded *blanqueamiento* (whitening) as the solution to racial disparities. *Blanqueamiento* was often regarded as a necessary part of the process toward the creation of the revolutionary Afro-Cuban "new man." Afro-Cuban leaders and intellectuals who within the context of the Cuban Revolution tried to promote racial issues and criticize racial inequities were often treated harshly, as the cases of Walterio Carbonell, Dr. Edualdo Gutiérrez Paula, Juán Betancourt Bencomo, Manuel Granados and many others bear out. They either lost their jobs, had publications withdrawn from circulation, were imprisoned, forced into exile, or a combination of these things.[11] *Negritud* was tolerated as long as it assumed its proper place within the orthodoxy of Marxist-Leninist doctrine and remained subservient to the class struggle. This contradictory relationship with Afro-Cuban culture was part of the context during which criticism of the schools developed. Remarkably, critics of the "hypothetical Afro-Cuban origins" of Porro's School of Plastic Arts claimed that much of the memory of Africa had been "erased by slavery," so any architectural representation thereof was artificial. This bias was primarily rooted in the traditional Creole prejudice against *negrismo*, but nevertheless supported by orthodox Marxist ideology. Some Cuban intellectuals, both in and out of Cuba, play down the contradictions of race, claiming that issues of nationalism have always taken precedence over those of race in Cuba. There is a tendency, even among some of the best intentioned of these intellectuals, to sometimes regard Afro-Cuban culture in an almost "Orientalist" framework. It is interesting to note that as the Soviet Union sought to establish a cultural policy reflecting the ethnic "other" of its eastern republics. Much of this policy, too, was ultimately "Orientalist" in nature.[12]

In 1962 there had been an incident in which Wifredo Lam and his use of Afro-Cuban imagery had briefly been subject to a formal and ideological critique that was not unlike that which descended upon the schools. Lam had been abroad during the October

Wifredo Lam, Quarto Famba, *1947*
(PRIVATE COLLECTION, MIAMI)

Crisis (Missle Crisis). Rivals of his took this opportunity to attack him upon his return to Cuba and brand him and his art as "counterrevolutionary." This would not be the first or last example of ideology being martialled to pursue personal feuds in Cuba. Ricardo Porro and Carlos Franqui, editor of *Revolution*, hastily organized an exhibition and the publication of a catalog, to which Porro provided the text (see Documents), in order to defend Lam's reputation as an artist and revolutionary. Ironically, Lam, who died in Paris in 1982, went on to become one of Cuba's most respected and untouchable cultural figures. Porro and Franqui became exiles.

In 1963 there was another move against "counterrevolutionary" art that probably also had as much to do with personal as well as ideological issues, and it too illustrates the generally contentious atmosphere. The works attacked represented some of the most formally avant-garde in Cuba. Largely upon the instigation of powerful PSP member Edith García Buchaca, a year before her downfall, a large work by Tomás Oliva, which had won a prize at the São Paolo Bienal, was removed from the Teatro Blanquito. A mural by Guido Llinás in Maceo Park was also attacked as "counterrevolutionary" in a denunciation lead by Osmany Cienfuegos. And in another act by Edith García Buchaca, a mural in the Naval Hospital by Hugo Consuegra was completely destroyed. For whatever reasons, the avant-garde and the experimental in certain kinds of art were not particularly welcome.

Similarly, some themes were not particularly welcome in architecture. Sensuality and sexuality had been recurrent themes in Cuban art and literature for years. And in some of Cuba's architecture, from the Baroque to Art Deco to modern works, one can point to many examples of sensuous forms. But sexuality as overtly expressed in the School of Plastic Arts was foreign to architecture. It came into conflict with a puritanical tendency among some Cuban Communists that was not without basis. Havana had been a "sin city" for tourists prior to the Revolution, and the civic sexuality of its brothels and live sex shows represented a decadent capitalist past to be buried for good. On the other hand, the victory of the Revolution was a catharsis of sorts that released the tensions and fears under which many had been living during the final years of the armed struggle, resulting in a (hetero)sexual revolution that some of the leaders thought was getting out of hand. In the general libidinous ambiance, "sex was in the air everywhere," noted one informant nostalgically. Moreover, for the former combatants, the libertine city life contrasted sharply with the austerity of their former guerrilla existence. Che Guevara, ever the moralist, finding himself helpless to prevent his men from sneaking out of their barracks at night for a romp with girlfriends, sought to remedy the situation by imposing a mass wedding for his troops in the futile hope that this might curb his boys from being boys. These conditions may account for part of the context for criticism of the schools' "sensuality" equating it with degeneracy. It is amusing to note that water was banned for a period from Porro's suggestive fountain, on Party orders. Criticism of the school's sensuality adhered to the political rhetoric of the times:

> If sensuality—whether originating in Africa or in the tropics—corresponds to the erotic world that comes from leisure, the contemplative life, and coincides with thoughtless impulse, [the result is] irrationalism; the representative spirit of the Revolution is the total antithesis: rigor imposed by the struggle against the enemy, hard and tenacious work necessary to rise from underdevelopment, scientific education necessary to dominate available resources and to design the society of the future—these require active social integration and not individual contemplative isolation.[13]

An awkward thread of logic leads from sensuality to deviance. One of the informal but damaging charges endured by the architects was that the school's curvilinear forms indicated homosexual tendencies. This was no casual accusation. The Cuban Revolution was marked by machismo and intense homophobia that, beginning in 1961, had on several occasions resulted in the police round-up of scores of gay Cubans who were sent off to "reeducation" camps. By 1965 this persecution had extended to the university and to the school of architecture. Though this policy was later officially repudiated, it nevertheless formed part of the context in which criticism of the schools developed, when innuendo concerning one's sexual orientation could be disastrous to one's career.[14]

The short film *PM* by Sabá Cabrera Infante and Orlando Jiménez-Leal was condemned for its sensuality in 1961, as construction on the art schools was commencing. The trial and banning of this film, as well as the later suppression of the cultural review *Lunes de Revolución*, are part of the context of the later repression of the art schools. The seemingly harmless twenty-minute film was a neorealist celebration of the sensual, rough and tumble, nightlife of Havana's gritty waterfront bars. The film was condemned during three hearings held at the National Library in June 1961, the same month in which Fidel Castro praised the art schools. Castro himself took a leading part in the hearings. Among other things, *PM* was accused of being too "sexy" and of misrepresenting the Revolution by portraying "too many Afro-Cubans." Alfredo Guevara, the head of Cuba's new film institute denounced *PM* as "counterrevolutionary and decadent."[15] *Lunes de Revolución*, which had been a font of revolutionary cultural energy, was closed the following October on the grounds of promoting "degeneracy." The extreme formalized procedures taken against *PM* and *Lunes de Revolución*, were not taken against the art schools, however, when they fell from grace three years later. There were no hearings. They were never officially banned or suppressed, just criticized and allowed to fade away.

In October 1964, Fidel Castro gave a general address to the country's architects and engineers. It was the year after Cuba had received its first prefabricated building system, the *Gran Panel*, from the Soviet Union and three years after he had praised the National Art Schools as "the most beautiful academy of arts in the world." In this characteristically long speech, Castro addressed many issues such as agricultural production, education and socialist principles. Regarding construction, Castro stressed the need for economy, though he cautioned those gathered not to sacrifice quality and form. He said that he agreed with the Soviet solution of standardized construction in an effort to achieve these ends. He also criticized the "egocentric criteria" of some architects who "pretend to make a particular case out of every building,"[16] an indirect repudiation of the National Arts Schools and their architects. Castro's words now echoed those of Nikita Khrushchev who a decade earlier had criticized Soviet architects who "follow the example of masters of architecture and wish to design only buildings of an individual character, and are in a hurry to build monuments to themselves."

During the informal campaign against the National Art Schools and their architects, there were several public attempts to defend them from attacks. In fact, in the same month as Castro's critical speech, a very positive article by Darío Carmona titled "Dos Ciudades de la Imaginación—Escuelas de Arte de La Habana," appeared in *Cuba*, a sort of revolutionary *Life* magazine. It was largely a photo essay with comments by foreign critics, and in what was probably a nationalistic prejudice, portrayed and mentioned only the work of Ricardo Porro. In it was an interesting comment by Graham Greene on the School of Plastic Arts:

> [T]he sculpture and painting studios are the work of a young architect, Ricardo Porro. They appear as an African village built of brick. Each house has its own domed roof and little streets circulate, meandering from one school to the other. All of a sudden streams of water burst forth and at each bend the perspective is different. It is like a village hidden in the hills. And this reminds the visitor that Cuba is as African as it is Spanish, and that the African has finally been liberated. . . . Segregation has ended.[17]

The following year Mario Coyula Cowley wrote supportively of the schools in an article entitled "Cuban Architecture, its History and its Possibilities," in the international edition of *Cuba Revolution and Culture*.

> The architects undertook their work eager to achieve a visual effect in harmony with the landscape and Cuban cultural tradition. They labored with great precision, helped by the characteristics of the project. Although not fully completed, the ensemble is very impressive by its size and freedom of form which at moments produces an almost sensational effect. Adding to this, the charm of other elements, not of apparent necessity, it is easily understood that the project—carried out in an economically poor country under constant threat of invasion—is the Cuban architectural achievement which is best known abroad. Among Cuban architects it is a constant object of discussion and the symbol of an attitude and a differentiating element which divides them into "tecnicistas" and "humanistas."[18]

The most supportive and comprehensive defense of the National Arts Schools was presented by Hugo Consuegra in a well-illustrated article with photographs by Paolo Gasparini in the pages of the journal *Arquitectura Cuba* in 1965. (See "Documents" for a complete transcript.) It was to be the last attempt of this period to reconcile the schools within the values of the Cuban Revolution and salvage their reputation. Consuegra, both an accomplished artist and architect, was an important part of Havana's cultural world. From 1953 to 1955 he had been a leading member of an group of avant-garde abstract painters known as Los Once. He had also been a founding member of Arquitectos Unidos and had been active in anti-Batista activities. With the Revolution he became Director of the Department of Fine Arts of the Ministry of Public Works until 1963. At the time he wrote this article he was a professor of art history in the school of architecture in Havana.

Consuegra's article makes for very interesting reading because of the terms of his argument and how it is presented (see full text in Documents). He begins with the charges that the schools are "out of scale" with Cuba's needs and represent an "excess and grandiloquence" incompatible with revolutionary values, to which he responded, implicitly defending them against charges of excessive cost:

> What is one to think of a small underdeveloped country just ninety miles from the United States that declares itself the "first socialist country in America?" A small country whose economy, production and markets were entirely controlled and organically dependent upon its colossal enemy, and dares to break this dependence and live in perpetual threat. David and Goliath! Out of scale, without a doubt.

and

> [I]s it not grandiloquent and spectacular our historic moment? . . . If Cuban
> culture—in any of its manifestations—aspires to reflect the Revolution, I
> estimate that it must do so fully aware of a certain excessiveness; meaning:
> freely indiscreet and shockingly realistic. . . . The National Art Schools,
> above and beyond the personal expression of their creators—two Italian
> architects and one Cuban—are the expression of this moment in revolution-
> ary Cuba.[19]

He uses a similar strategy with the accusation that the architects were
"cultural aristocrats," repackaging it as a positive attribute. Like others
during the period, he indulges in a bit of revolutionary hyperbole:

> It is not important whether the architects of these works are Cuban or
> foreign, they are, by their architectural formation and work, true "cultural
> aristocrats": humanist architects, products of the whole complexity of
> contemporary culture. It is well understood that these "aristocrats" are faith-
> ful to the Revolution, they march shoulder to shoulder with the people to
> harvest cane and they stand guard rifle in hand.[20]

Much of the rest of Consuegra's article is a description and analysis
of the schools. He deals with all of the schools and each architect equally,
unlike so many other writings which tend to single out Porro. His descrip-
tions of the schools are quite insightful and the most articulate found in
any Cuban publication. Consuegra pays particular attention to formal
disintegration as he finds it in the design of all the schools and how this
is used to convey a sense of spatial anxiety. He analyzes the role of the
paseo arquitectónico in maintaining the visitor in a disoriented state,
and how all these formal complexities correctly and positively communi-
cate Cuba's revolutionary ethos of the moment. Consuegra ends on an
positive note:

> I am optimistic in respect to the future of these works. Reality—as hard as it
> can be now—and hope—as fantastic as it might seem—are converging, all the
> time more vertiginously in revolutionary Cuba. Abundance will unfailingly
> come. The "disproportion" of the schools of art will diminish with time.

But Consuegra's optimism proved to be "out of scale," both for the
National Art Schools as well as for the future of Cuba itself. Also, part of
his article had been censored, a paragraph in which he referred to the
October Crisis (Missile Crisis). Consuegra recalls:

[The form in which] it was published alludes to the Cuban/Soviet disagreement during the October Crisis and the withdrawal of the missiles. The original form was more direct—calling the missiles by their name—and italicizing [the words] "total independence." This was the dream of independence that many of us—intellectuals and political leaders—had in those days: the possibility of creating a "camino cubano," different from the "caminos 'yankee' y 'soviético.'"[21]

One could argue that this small, though loaded, change in text and emphasis was more a case of editing than censoring. But either way, the motive for the change was clearly political. Eventually, Hugo Consuegra found himself too intellectually confined by the increasingly restrictive environment. In 1966 he felt compelled to leave Cuba for Spain. In 1970 Consuegra moved to New York where he practiced architecture and painted until his death in 2003.

Consuegra's carefully constructed defense of the National Art Schools did little to alter their fate. While Roberto Gottardi and Vittorio Garatti sought to adapt themselves to the changing political environment and work within the new architectural norms in Cuba, Ricardo Porro refused to relinquish his principles regarding an autochthonous, organic, provocative, and revolutionary architecture.[22] Earlier in 1963 he had been criticized for "escapist tendencies" for lecturing on Frank Lloyd Wright and assigning readings from Heinrich Wölflin to his students instead of encouraging them to immerse themselves in proletarian reality. Porro had also been an outspoken critic of the purges in the architecture school and the persecution of gays. He therefore bore the brunt of the criticism of the art schools in both its official and unofficial manifestations which at times approached the bizarre. Often he woke up in the morning to find very unscientific forms of criticism waiting for him in his garden—decapitated chickens, powders carefully wrapped in colored paper and other objects of *santería*. But in the end, this was all overshadowed by what had become an intractable situation, as Porro recalls:

There were those in the Ministry who made my life impossible, a daily struggle. Then came the purges in the university which I was very much against. Then there were the persecutions of the gays which I was very much against. But in the end I do not accuse anybody. I cannot blame individuals. You have to understand the context. The passions of the moment obscured rational thought and common sense. Moreover, you have to understand the true impersonal nature of repression. It is a Kafkaesque drama in which you do not know who charges you or who judges you—it just happens. And you are made to feel very guilty, like original sin, even though you did nothing.

LEFT TO RIGHT: Ricardo Porro, Carlos Lechuga, Dr. Osvaldo Dorticós Torrado, Roberto Gottardi, and unidentified mason inspecting the schools (UNKNOWN PHOTOGRAPHER)

Finally, Fidel personally intervened to see what the problem was all about. He sent [President Osvaldo] Dorticós and another minister, Carlos Lechuga to investigate and report to him on the situation of the schools, and he realized that my persecution was in error. Carlos Rafael [Rodríguez] was very supportive too, and he, like Fidel, did what he could to help me. But in the eyes of the Ministry I was banned—*prohibido*. As a consequence, my name later disappeared from my work. This, like the removal of certain individuals from photographs, is unfortunately a common occurrence in socialist countries. Nevertheless, Fidel offered to transfer me to another ministry. But I knew that there would be no more opportunities to make architecture in which I believed. In the end Fidel was very generous, he understood the situation. He had his secretary Celia Sánchez arrange for my departure.[23]

In July 1966 Ricardo Porro, with his wife and son, and little more than two paintings by Wifredo Lam, departed for Paris, to a new life and a new career. Vittorio Garatti would depart too, but much later. In June 1974 he was arrested and imprisoned for twenty-one days on charges of espionage. Even though he was acquitted, he was expelled from the country, and he returned to Milan where he started a practice. Of the three architects, only Roberto Gottardi remained. It was considered necessary to reorient others who had worked on the schools. Heriberto Duverger who had worked on the schools as a young architecture student would recall many years later:

> Due to the violent reaction generated during its erection, the temple of the new faith, "Las Escuelas Nacionales de Arte" was declared finished in its unfinished state. The student designers who took part in the project, declared outlaws and enemies of the truth, were scandalously dispersed among the technical productive units of the Ministry of Construction to help them get their feet back on the ground. As soon as the principal architects, priests of this religion, had been successfully neutralized and subjected to a bloody

process of marginalization, we reached an equilibrium in which the law and reeducation would be imposed by the winner. Peace and the centrality of the technosphere were restored. Work was organized within the centralized culture. "Creativity" was discouraged.[24]

The repudiation of the National Art Schools represented an important symbolic step in the consolidation of power in the hands of MICONS by July 26, 1965, the date the schools were declared officially opened and work was definitively suspended. Just prior to that, in March, the architecture faculty had been placed firmly under the control of MICONS. The director of the school, Roberto Carrazana, had been replaced by the vice minister of MICONS, Eduardo Granados. The head of the design program, Fernando Salinas, himself no friend of the art schools or Porro, had nevertheless been replaced by Antonio Quintana.[25] In his new capacity, one of Quintana's first directives to the faculty was to forbid them to allow their students to visit the art schools. Moreover, Quintana, who had provoked much of the opposition to the art schools from within MICONS, now positioned himself to become the Cuban Revolution's "court architect." Until his death in 1993 he used his political skills to secure a near monopoly over major public commissions, which unfortunately represent a rather undistinguished body of work, despite the design freedom uniquely accorded to him. He was successful, however, in denying these opportunities to other architects who were left to contend with restrictive, standardized norms. This increased authority within the hands of MICONS mirrored activities that were occurring elsewhere. Centralization was occurring at the highest levels of the Cuban government. On October 3, 1965, the Partido Comunista de Cuba (PCC) was formally inaugurated, replacing and consolidating the power of the former PURS, which had incorporated cadre from the former July 26 Movement, the Revolutionary Directorate, and the PSP.

As for the course architecture was to take, Mario Coyula Cowley, architect and current deputy director of the Grupo de Desarollo Integral de la Capital summed it up in the following:

> While a self-serving *apparat* became more and more involved in its own maintenance, the social role of the architect was devalued in relation to other professions. The purpose of an architect's education was not to stimulate creativity and invite change, but to maintain an existing system, an establishment that promoted endlessly repetitive projects, based on rigid pre-fabricated systems. The people who could have been important in changing things were too often compromised themselves in the maintenance of the establishment, or felt helpless to promote change and shifted their efforts to planning, writing, teaching or other activities. Critics of real substance were rare and often fell

into a kind of self-censorship. For the architect it became convenient to sacrifice beauty in order to guarantee the quantity of production. Life has shown that when you sacrifice beauty, you lose everything: social value, quality of construction and in the end also quantity.[26]

Coyula's words are given historical resonance by those of Berthold Lubetkin, who, reflecting back on the course of Soviet architecture, wrote:

> Disarming itself by rejecting the whole of past architectural tradition, the profession gradually lost all confidence in itself and in its social purpose. Those architects who were most honest with themselves drew their own conclusion from the worship of the engineer and the denial of all architectural tradition, and actually abandoned their profession to become building technicians, administrators and planners.[27]

With the adoption of Soviet-style conformity and centralized models, a chapter closed in the history of Cuban architecture. The search for an architectural *cubanidad* that would reflect the identity of an Afro-Hispanic, Caribbean, socialist society—effectively came to an end. The National Art Schools themselves were allowed to fall into various states of decay. Once objects of pride, they were now treated with indifference and/or embarrassment. Porro's two schools, Modern Dance and Plastic Arts, were complete as originally conceived, save some miscellaneous interior work. Both are utilized today but haphazardly maintained, and Clara Porcet's cabinetry and woodwork in both have sadly disappeared or been destroyed. Roberto Gottardi's partially constructed School of Dramatic Arts is occupied but underutilized and poorly maintained, with one section in ruins. Like the theater in Gottardi's school, the performance halls of Vittorio Garatti's School of Music were left unbuilt, and today only a third of the constructed school is used. The remainder is abandoned and left to ruin.

Most incomprehensible is the total abandonment and progressive decay of Garatti's School of Ballet. It was 90% complete when work on it was terminated. Alicia Alonso, the director of the school, both participated in and approved of all phases of the project. During a visit when the school was almost complete, however, she reportedly took one last look, saying "*No me gusta,*" and left, never to return. Was this a spontaneous expression of her taste, or a self-preserving response to the growing restrictive ideological environment? Either way, the classical ballerina thereupon appropriated a classical colonial mansion in El Vedado to house her school, where it remains today. Garatti's Ballet School was briefly used for training circus performers, then abandoned. Today it serves as a kind of quarry for scavengers in search of building materials. Its mahogany *medio puntos* have been completely stripped. Bricks and tiles also continue to disappear from the school, now engulfed in a magic realist, tropical, Piranesean landscape.

In 1979, in an affront that further symbolized architectural hegemony of MICONS, a crude concrete slab dormitory, constructed of prefabricated panels, was erected facing Ricardo Porro's School of Plastic Arts.

In reflecting back over the contentious history of the National Art Schools, Roberto Gottardi has said:

> We began the schools with the belief that all was possible. There was so much faith in the future at that time and a complete lack of preconceived ideas. This perhaps eventually took the schools somewhere that was economically out of scale with their ambitions. But was this any reason for the absurd attacks suffered by the architects? . . . Nevertheless, the euphoria, enthusiasm, unbounded happiness . . . that is what I believe is most reflected in the schools. That is still today their greatest message.[28]

NOTES

1. Jorge G. Castañeda, *Utopia Unarmed: The Latin American Left after the Cold War*, (New York, Vintage Books, 1994): 74.

2. Lisandro Otero, interview quoted in: Castañeda, Ibid., 185.

3. Ricardo Porro, interview with the author (November 1997).

4. Nikita Khrushchev, "Remove Shortcomings in Design, Improve Work of Architects," in Joan Ockman, *Architecture Culture 1943–1968* (New York: Columbia Books of Architecture), 185–186.

5. Roberto Segre and Rafael López Rangel, *Architettura e territorio nell'America Latina. Saggi & Documenti* (Milan: Electa Editrice, 1982), 224 (author's translation). See also López Rangel's summation of the criticism in Documents, herein.

6. A chronological reading of Segre's books and articles, published from 1968 to 1996, reveals a fairly consistent critical position toward the schools until 1993. In this year Segre expressed a supportive view of just the two schools by Vittorio Garatti. By 1996 he was favorably disposed toward all five. These texts reflect both an evolution of Segre's analysis as well as an evolution of the political and cultural context in Cuba itself. For our purposes, it is the earlier texts that serve to best illustrate the ideological context against which the schools and their architects ran aground (see Bibliography).

7. Roberto Segre and Rafael López Rangel, op. cit. (author's translation).

8. It is interesting to note that in the 1950s, Cuban architect Manuel Gutiérrez experimented with economical, innovative constructive techniques that included prefabrication. He, like most of his colleagues, left for the U.S., and his creative body of work was not used as a base upon which to build an appropriate industrialized Cuban technology.

9. Roberto Segre, *Diez Años de Arquitectura Revolucionaria en Cuba* (Havana: Ediciones Union, 1969), 87 (author's translation). These criticisms are notably absent in Segre's most recent publication in which the schools now receive a sympathetic review. "La Habana siglo XX: espacio dilatado y tiempo contraído," *Ciudad y Territorio, Estudios Territoriales* XXVIII (110), 1996.

10. Aldo van Eyck, as quoted in Joan Ockman, *Architecture Culture 1943–1968* (New York: Columbia Books of Architecture), 347.

11. Carbonell, a Marxist historian and ethnologist, author of *Birth of a National Culture* (banned in 1961), and former diplomat for the revolutionary government, was imprisoned for criticizing racial inequities. Gutiérrez, a journalist, and opponent of the Batista regime was likewise suppressed for publicly criticizing the absence of Afro-Cubans in the upper ranks of the revolutionary government. Betancourt, former national president of the Sociedades de Color, Afro-Cuban mutual aid societies, was forced into exile after the societies were closed down by the government. Granados, a writer, likewise chose exile in Paris, where he died in 1998. For an examination of issues of race in Cuba since the Revolution see Ronald Segal, "The Roads of Cuba," chapter 20 of *The Black Diaspora, Five Centuries of the Black Experience* (New York: Farrar, Strauss, and Giroux, 1995), 224–243, and Carlos Moore, *Castro, the Blacks and Africa* (Los Angeles: Center for Afro-American Studies, UCLA, 1998) with introduction by Jorge Domínguez.

12. For an analysis of the Soviet Union's contradictory relationship with the culture and architecture of its eastern republics see: Greg Castillo, "Soviet Orientalism: Socialist Realism and Built Tradition," *Traditional Dwellings and Settlements Review* VII, no. 11 (Spring 1997): 33–47.

13. R. Segre, *Diez Años de Arquitectura Revolucionaria en Cuba*, (Havana: Ediciones Union, 1969), 89 (author's translation).

14. There was no doubt as to the gendering of the "New Man" in Cuba or elsewhere in the socialist world, as documented in: Greg Castillo and Jan Plamper, "*Homo Sovieticus* vs. the Homosexuals: A Study in the Socialist Construction of Deviance," University of California at Berkeley, unpublished paper.

15. Another interesting episode for comparison is that of the joint Soviet/Cuban production of the film *Yo Soy Cuba*, directed by Mikhail Kalatozov, written by Yevgeny Yevtushenko and Enrique Pineda Barnet. Begun just before the October Crisis this delirious piece of *agit-prop* took great delight in portraying the sensual and decadent world of Havana before the Revolution. Stuart Klawans described it in the *Nation* (March 20, 1995) as "a fabulous beast of a movie, part white elephant and part fire-breathing dragon. . . ." Like the art schools, this film, considered bordering on "degeneracy" also disappeared, but into the shelves of the archives of the Moscow Film Institute, only to be rediscovered and restored by Francis Ford Coppola and Martin Scorsese in 1995.

16. F. Castro, "Closing speech to the First Congress of Cuban Builders," October 25, 1964, as quoted in Susana Torre, "Architecture and Revolution: Cuba, 1959 to 1974," *Progressive Architecture*, (October 1974): 89. Interestingly enough, Castro's position reversed itself in 1995 when he praised

the highly conceptual and individual urban design proposals for Havana by architects Coop Himmelb(l)au, Morphosis/Thom Mayne, Eric Owen Moss, Carme Pinós, Lebbeus Woods, and CPPN in his introductory statement to *The Havana Project, Architecture Again*, edited by Peter Noever.

17. Graham Greene, quoted in Darío Carmona, "Dos Ciudades de la Imaginación—Escuelas de Arte de La Habana," *Cuba* 30 (3 October 1964): 38.

18. M. Coyula Cowley, "Cuban Architecture its History and its Possibilities," *Cuba Revolution and Culture* 2 (1965): 12–25.

19. Hugo Consuegra, "Las Escuelas Nacionales de Arte," *Arquitectura Cuba* 334 (1965): 15.

20. Ibid., 16.

21. Hugo Consuegra, unpublished memoirs, 1998. (author's translation). In the characteristic Cuban penchant for finding humor in even the most unpleasant of situations, Consuegra and the editor, after arguing, together joked: "Cuba was against withdrawing the missiles from the island. But we withdrew the missiles from the article." Ibid.

22. Ricardo Porro, ever maintaining a provocative position, submitted an entry for a monument to the Revolution in Levisa that consisted of a group of Olmec-scaled heads at the foot of a monumental guillotine.

23. R. Porro, interview with the author (November 1997). It is interesting that while repression can have an "impersonal nature," protection can have a very personal nature. While Fidel Castro's address of October 1964 was implicitly critical of the National Art Schools and their architects, he for whatever reasons did not subject Ricardo Porro to the level of repression that some other independently minded cultural figures had to endure. Fidel Castro and Ricardo Porro were social acquaintances within a closely knit, and very Cuban, network of friends. Castro and Elena Porro's brother had been close friends in law school, for example. In the end there is an intimacy as well as a fragility to an *apparat* which responds to impulses that are often other than political. As for Osvaldo Dorticós, he served as Cuba's president until the First Party Congress in December 1975. In 1983 he committed suicide.

24. Heriberto Duverger, "Mis Años Felices," unpublished article, 1992.

25. This had been precipitated by an interesting chain of events. In mid March 1965 the architecture faculty and students, seventy in total, temporarily abandoned their academic activities to form two brigades of volunteers to do agricultural work in the south of Matanzas. The women's brigade was assigned to pick potatoes. The men's brigade was to plant sugarcane. During a break for political discussion, a group of more radical students aggressively criticized their less politicized peers for errors of, among other things: formalism, bourgeois orientation, and homosexual tendencies. There had already been accusations circulating in the school against members who were perceived as homosexuals or otherwise "disaffected" from the revolutionary process. The motive was to "purge" the school of these undesirables. Realizing that things were getting out of hand, the director Roberto Carrazana along with Iván Espín and Osmundo Machado Ventura called a halt to the divisive discourse that was ensuing in the men's work brigade. But within two days of their return to Havana, a general meeting of faculty and students was called by Armando Hart, who berated the faculty for their petty bourgeois tendencies. Immediately, after this Carrazana and Salinas (who had carefully avoided the controversy) were sacked. Ironically, Hart himself later gave Salinas a sinecure within the Ministry of Culture, which he held until his death in 1993. Espín and Machado Ventura were spared because they both had family connections to revolutionary leaders. The professors considered too "intellectually oriented," Fofi Fernández, Vittorio Garatti, Roberto Gottardi, Joaquín Rallo and Roberto Segre were sent to work in different areas of "production" to acquaint them better with proletarian reality. In Rallo's case, as mentioned earlier, this tragically and unnecessarily lead to his death.

26. Mario Coyula Cowley, interview with the author (1993). For further information on how architecture developed in from the beginning of the Cuban Revolution to the early 1990s see: John A. Loomis, "Architecture or Revolution?—The Cuban Experiment," *Design Book Review* (Summer 1994): 71–80.

27. Berthold Lubetkin, "Soviet Architecture: Notes on Development from 1917 to 1932," *Architectural Association Journal* (1956).

28. R. Gottardi, interview with the author (June 1992).

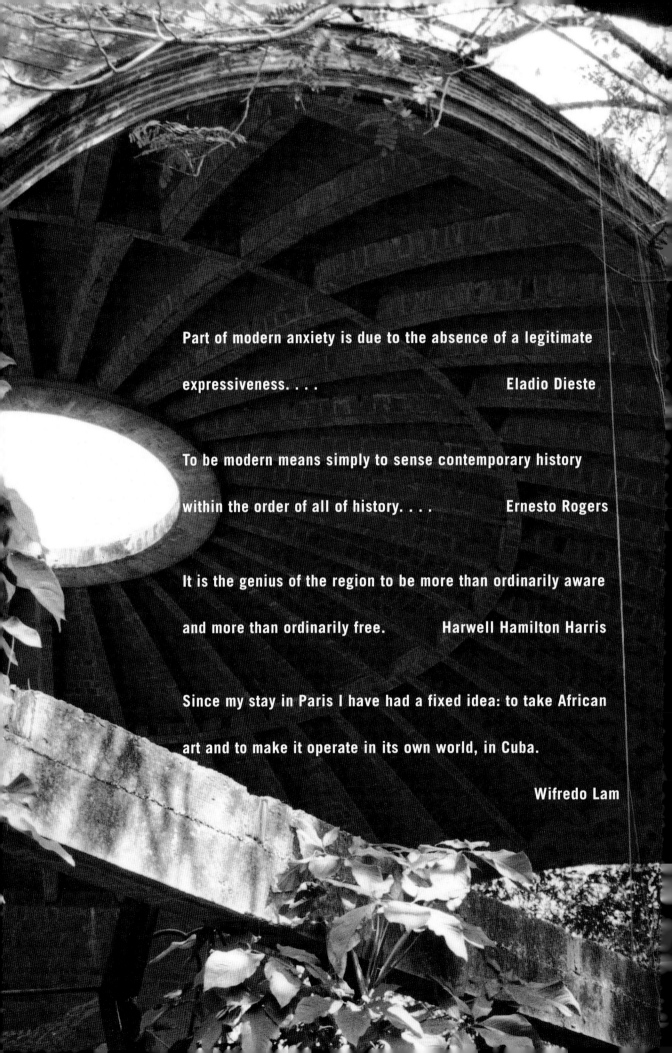

Part of modern anxiety is due to the absence of a legitimate

expressiveness. . . .   Eladio Dieste

To be modern means simply to sense contemporary history

within the order of all of history. . . .   Ernesto Rogers

It is the genius of the region to be more than ordinarily aware

and more than ordinarily free.   Harwell Hamilton Harris

Since my stay in Paris I have had a fixed idea: to take African

art and to make it operate in its own world, in Cuba.

                                                  Wifredo Lam

FIVE

Other Modernisms

The hegemony of modern architecture's rationalist tendency was first established by Siegfried Giedion and Nikolaus Pevsner. It was further typified in stylistic terms by Henry Russell Hitchcock and Philip Johnson. These critics could never really comfortably contend with the works of architects such as Hugo Häring, Eric Mendelsohn or Hans Scharoun, not to mention the likes of Frank Lloyd Wright, all of whom practiced on the margins of mainstream modern architecture. It was only after World War II that skepticism toward technocentric machine-age rationalism began to emerge, in part as a response to the horrors that technology had unleashed during that war. Nevertheless, Le Corbusier's heretical organic forms of the chapel at Ronchamp (1954) would provoke a crisis among the still numerous adherents of rationalism.

The actual origins of so called "organic" architecture, however, reach farther back into history. They can be found in the writings of William Morris where he used the term for the first time to refer to the Gothic, as well as the architecture he hoped it would inspire—"an architecture that would throw off the encumbrances of applied style and evolve its forms in the spirit of strict truthfulness, following the conditions of its use, material and construction."[1] The subsequent English Free Style, in the second half of the nineteenth century followed in this spirit, drawing from regional traditions. The "conditions of use" that were of greatest importance to Theodor Fischer, grandfather of German organic or "expressionist" architecture, were those of site and context. His greatest influence was academic, however. Hugo Häring, Hans Poelzig, Eric Mendelsohn, Bruno Taut, and Lois Welzenbacher were all his students. One of Fischer's only existing built works, the Post Office (1910) at Hall near Innsbruck, demonstrates the importance he attached to *genius loci*. While his German students went on to be associated with expressionism, Welzenbacher and other Austrians would initiate a particular regional autochthonous tendency in the Tyrol. Despite their relatively marginal place in recorded architectural history, these tendencies have continued to be a critical force, from the Philhar-

LEFT: *Hans Scharoun, Berlin Philharmonic Hall, 1957-63*
FROM V. LETI MESSINA, HANS SCHAROUN *(OFFICINA EDIZIONI, 1968)*
RIGHT: *Giovanni Michelucci, Church of San Giovanni Battista, Campi Bisenzio (Florence), 1964*
FROM F. DAL CO, STORIA DELL'ARCHITETTURA ITALIANA *(ELECTA, 1997)*

monic Hall (Berlin, 1957–63) by Hans Scharoun (1893–1972) to the more current work of Coop Himmelb(l)au.

Organic architecture was part of the search for architectural alternatives for which Italy served as a crucible during the postwar years. Bruno Zevi, who had spent the years during World War II studying architecture in the U.S. and had become very much influenced by the work of Frank Lloyd Wright, returned to Italy shortly following its liberation to proselytize for organic architecture. In 1953 he published his polemical treatise, *La Poetica dell'architettura neoplastica*. Shortly thereafter he formed the Association for Organic Architecture (APAO), which would attempt to extend the integrative argument for the organic into the broader cultural and political arena. In addition to Zevi, architects such as Mario Ridolfi, Ludovico Quaroni, Giuseppe Samonà and Carlo Scarpa also in the 1950s contributed to Italy's architectural diversity through their practices and teaching. In the Ticino region of Italy and Switzerland in the 1950s there was a similar organic tendency. Kenneth Frampton points out that architecture during those years

> was oriented towards the work of Frank Lloyd Wright rather than the pre-war Italian Rationalists. Of this period Tita Carloni wrote: "We naively set ourselves the objective of an 'organic' Ticino, in which the values of modern culture were to be interwoven in a natural way with local tradition."[2]

Practice in Ticino later shifted again in the 1960s, favoring rationalist, though regionalist, roots which ultimately proved to be the dominant influence, effectively integrating local tradition and the vernacular as exhibited later on by the work of Mario Botta and others. Nevertheless, this Ticinese episode of the 1950s is interesting in the way it parallels regionalist concerns elsewhere. In Italy, Carlo Scarpa (1906-78) continued to provide provocative examples, far from the mainstream, of an architecture rooted in material, constructive technique and place. In 1964 the

ABOVE: *Banfi, Belgiojoso, Peressutti and Rogers, Torre Velasca, Milan, 1958*
FROM S. MAFFIOLETTI, BBPR, (ZANICHELLI, 1994)

much acclaimed Church of San Giovanni Battista by Giovanni Michelucci (1891-1990) reproposed the organic alternative in Italy.

One of the most important critics during the revisionist years of the 1950s in Italy was Ernesto Nathan Rogers (1909-69). Rogers proposed the reintroduction of history and context into architectural design. He advocated this progressive integration of history and a respect for the continuity of *preesistenze ambientali* (preexisting environmental conditions or context) through his teaching at the Politécnico di Milano, his practice with Banfi, Belgiojoso, Peressutti and Rogers (BBPR) and through his editorship of *Casabella-continuità* from 1953-64. Projects such as the Torre Velasca (1958) and the Piazza Meda Office Building (1969) represent BBPR's efforts to create a modern architecture sensitive to history and context. For Rogers, modernism represented not a break with history, but a part of a larger process of historical continuity.

> Many of those considered innovators share with the so-called conservators the common flaw that they start from formal prejudices, maintaining that the new and the old are opposed rather than represent the dialectical continuity of the historical process; both are limited, in fact, to the idolatry of certain styles frozen into a few images, and they are incapable of penetrating the essences that are pregnant with inexhaustible energies. To pretend to build in a preconceived "modern style" is as absurd as to demand respect for the taboo of past styles.[3]

This position was very threatening to committed rationalists who had been influenced by the Bauhaus's rejection of history. Reyner Banham attacked Rogers in the pages of *Architectural Review* in 1959, accusing him of betraying modernism in an editorial entitled "Neoliberty—the Italian Retreat from Modern Architecture," to which Rogers replied with an editorial of his own, sarcastically entitled "The Evolution of Architecture: Reply to the Custodian of Frigidaires." It is not an insignificant

LEFT: J. S. Coderch, ISM Apartment Block, Barcelona, Spain, 1951 *(FROM ZODIAC 5, 1959)*
CENTER: Jordi Bonet, Church of San Medi, Barcelona, Spain, 1960 *(AVERY LIBRARY, COLUMBIA UNIVERSITY)*
RIGHT: Carlos Mijares, San José Parochial Center, Jungapeo, Mexico, 1982 *(FROM ZODIAC 8, 1993)*

coincidence that all three architects of the National Art Schools had personally come into contact with the critical thinking of Rogers: Porro as a student at a seminar organized by CIAM in 1951, Garatti as a student at the Politécnico di Milano, and Gottardi as an employee at BBPR. Rogers's revisionist thought can be considered a sort of theoretical common denominator that helped to link the three architects. Nevertheless, Rogers's position was not widely appreciated and Vittorio Garatti remembers him as a marginalized figure on the faculty at the Politécnico di Milano.

On the other side of the Atlantic, deep in the heart of Texas, history was being introduced into the design instruction at the architecture school at the Univeristy of Texas at Austin through the efforts of Colin Rowe. He along with Bernhard Hoesli and others who later became known as the "Texas Rangers" were engaged in a restructuring of the curriculum during the years 1954-58 that would have later resonance throughout the U.S. History and context were to be cornerstones of this new pedagogy. These curricular reforms had been initiated during the deanship of Harwell Hamilton Harris (1903-1990) from 1951 to 1955. Prior to his Texas deanship, Harris along with William Wurster (1895-1973) represented a distinctive regionalist tendency in California. Their work also reflected the desire to reconfigure or redirect modern architecture away from universalist values toward an architecture informed by region, place and history. Both developed significant, yet diverse, bodies of work that emphasized wood, the local material of choice, with its constructive techniques and traditions. Much of the restrained and understated work of these two architects was eclipsed, however, in the mainstream publications by the work of Charles and Ray Eames, Richard Neutra, Gregory Ain and others

LEFT: *Rogelio Salmona, Quimbaya Gold Museum and City Center, Armenia* (RICARDO CASTRO)
CENTER: *Eladio Dieste, Church of Atlántide, Uruguay, 1960* (PAOLO GASPARINI, FROM ZODIAC 8, 1993)
RIGHT: *Walter Betancourt, Cultural Center of Velasco, Cuba, 1964-91* (JOHN A. LOOMIS)

whose crisp formalism fit more into the universalist modern genre. Harris's concerns for the cultural integrity of the region were most cogently expressed in theoretical terms in 1954 in a talk given to the Eugene, Oregon AIA entitled "Regionalism and Nationalism." Here he advocated a "Regionalism of Liberation" that allowed a unique cultural identity to emerge and express itself in architecture.[4]

Regionalism and the politics of cultural identity were also issues that continued to influence architecture in Catalonia (land of the eponymous vaults) long after Gaudí and in spite of the repression of Francisco Franco's fascism. Here an architecture of cultural affirmation, or resistance, had to face the contradiction of addressing the rectilinear values of the rationalism of the Republican era as well as those of a more free-form regionalism of vernacular origins. The conscious persistence of a brick tradition is seen both in the faceted planar facade of the J. A. Coderch's ISM apartment block (1951) as well as the sensuous Catalan vaulted forms of the church of San Medi (1960) by Jordi Bonet, both in Barcelona.

Architecture in Catalonia illustrates the importance of the link of materiality to regionalism. The deeply rooted masonry tradition in this region made the employment of brick craft both a political as well as practical decision. It is probably reasonable to generalize that strong regionalist tendencies in Catalonia often led the designer to choose locally produced, masonry building materials. While not a rationalist decision, this is a rational decision that allows materials to assume their proper constructive forms. The undulating masonry Catalan vault is no less rational than a rectilinear steel column-and-beam structure.

Hispanic, if not Catalan, masonry traditions were also sustained throughout various regions of Latin America in the diverse work of such

Other Modernisms

LEFT: *Félix Candela, Church of Our Miraculous Lady, Mexico City, Mexico, 1954*
FROM C. FABER, CANDELA: THE SHELL BUILDER (REINHOLD PUBLISHING CO, 1963)

CENTER: *Ricardo Porro, Competition project for a hotel, San Sebastián, Spain, 1963* (PAOLO GASPARINI)

RIGHT: *Salvador de Alba Martín, Market at San Juan de los Lagos, Jalisco, Mexico, 1967*
S. DE ALBA, FROM ARCHITETTURA E SOCIETÀ: L'AMERICA LATINA NEL XX SECOLO, (JACA BOOK, 1996)

architects as Antoni Bonet (Uruguay, 1913-89), Carlos Mijares (Mexico, b. 1930), Eduardo Sacriste (Argentina, b. 1905), Rogelio Salmona (Colombia, b. 1929) and Jimmy Alcock (Venezuela b. 1932). The work of engineer Eladio Dieste (Uruguay, b. 1917) continues to explore the plastic and tectonic potential of the brick as seen in the undulating walls of his Church of Atlántide (1960). In Cuba's eastern provinces, Walter Betancourt (1932-1978) successfully defied the Revolution's design conventions in his pursuit of Wrightian-influenced organic architecture using brick, most notably in the Forestry Research Laboratory at Guisa (1970) and the Cultural Center at Velasco (1964-1991).[5]

Just as the use of masonry does not imply organic form, the construction of organic forms does not necessarily require masonry technique. Félix Candela (b. 1910), a Spanish civil war emigrée architect, primarily based in Mexico, produced an abundance of projects throughout his career that were complex in form, ranging from hyperbolic paraboloids to folded plates, but rigorously determined by geometry. Projects such as the Church of La Virgin Milagrosa in Mexico City (1954) and the Church of San José Obrero in Monterrey (1959) were exclusively constructed in "modern" materials—reinforced concrete and ferrocement—but relied on the availability of low-cost labor more available in developing countries like Mexico. Organic form for Ricardo Porro could also manifest itself in reinforced concrete, but for him the formal determinant was a sculptural process, not a geometric one. His competition project for an exoskeletal structured hotel in San Sebastián, Spain (1963), although a radical departure from the forms of the National Art Schools, is nonetheless organic.

Other Latin American architects looked to traditional, low-tech, building techniques not so much as means of formal expression, but primarily as means to provide low-cost, quality solutions to the many building needs of the poor. In Mexico, Salvador de Alba Martín (b. 1926) used a variation of the Catalan vault technique in projects such as the Market at San Juan de los Lagos, Jalisco (1967). Fruto Vivas (b. 1928) experimented with adobe and wood structures in Venezuela. Miguel Ángel Bautista, María Eugenia Hurtaldo, Carlos González Lobo (Mexico), Edwin Quiles (Puerto Rico), and Victor Saúl Pelli (Argentina; brother of Cesar Pelli) represent just a few other architects who have devoted efforts to develop appropriate technologies and promote community participation. In another part of the developing world, Egyptian Hassan Fathy (1900-1989) had been advocating traditional techniques and vernacular form since the 1930s. His best known project of many is the new village of Gournah (1945-48) built with a mud brick vaulting technique which, like the Catalan vault, required no formwork. The efforts of these architects to seek low-tech building solutions for social needs were paralleled by similar efforts on the part of other advocates in the First World like Christopher Alexander and Lisa Peattie.

The vernacular was not only a source of constructive alternatives to modernist technology, but it also provided formal and linguistic opportunities that architects have employed since the elevation of the "primitive hut" in the eighteenth century. The vernacular has also been the major point of departure for much regionalist architecture. By 1953, even within CIAM, the vernacular was looked to, at least in theory, as a way out of the modern architecture's rationalist dilemma. In one of the reports published from the Aix-en-Provence meeting of that year, it was acknowledged that "a primitive Cameroon hut has more aesthetic dignity than most prefabricated houses."[6] In 1964 the prevailing interest and nostalgia toward the vernacular was illustrated in Bernard Rudofsky's *Architecture Without Architects*. While there was an active interest in the vernacular and local tradition among the more progressive and avant-garde architects in Cuba during the 1950s, these issues dropped out of the discourse with the consolidation of MICONS after the Revolution. Although Spanish colonial architecture was acknowledged by the revolutionary regime in Cuba as a part of the country's heritage, examples of the vernacular, such as the *bohio* peasant hut of indigenous Taino origin, were considered "backward," and any reference thereof was discouraged.

In further considering other modernisms, the relationship of the Modern Movement to Latin America bears examining. Le Corbusier is often simplisticly portrayed as the "Christopher Columbus" who brought modern architecture to the New World in 1929 and subsequent trips. The reality is of course much more complex. Many of the intellectual elites of Latin America were well-connected to their European counter-

ABOVE: *Oscar Niemeyer, Casino, Pampulha, 1942*
(PAOLO GASPARINI, FROM ZODIAC 8, 1993)

parts so that a blending of culture and discourse was natural. The first recognized work of modern architecture in Latin America, Rio's Ministry of Education (1936), is of contested parentage. The concept may be Corbu, but the hand is really that of the young Oscar Niemeyer (b. 1907). Much of Latin America's modern architecture sought diversity within the parameters of rationalist principles, while other examples sought to break out of those boundaries. On all accounts, Latin American modernism still manifested itself as a "white" architecture, but one that often transcended the formal bounds of rationalism. This "other" modernism was characterized by curvilinear forms, expressive freedom, and an affinity for the organic. Brazil's premier architect, also a Marxist, Niemeyer unabashedly attributes the sensuous forms found in his architecture to the influence of the curves of the Brazilian woman. Yet questions of parentage and the desire on the part of European and North American historians for Latin American architecture to validate its First World relatives, have endured. In 1948 Alberto Sartoris published his Italocentric *Encyclopédie de l'Architecture Nouvelle. Ordre et climat méditerranéens*, in which, by stressing the "Latin," he sought to link the new architecture with Mediterranean culture and classical heritage (to the exclusion of the Northern European and Anglo-Saxon relatives). But in time, some European critics would prove to be an unfaithful lot in regards to their postwar romance with Latin American modern architecture. This "other" modernism, for its expressive qualities, came to be regarded as deviant by some of the gatekeepers of orthodox Western European modern architecture. In 1954 in a series of articles entitled "Report on Brazil" in *Architectural Review*, Max Bill's comments could be considered almost racist:

There I saw some shocking things, modern architecture sunk to the depths, a riot of anti-social waste, lacking any sense of responsibility toward either the business occupant or his customers. . . . Here is utter anarchy in building, jungle growth in the worst sense.[7]

Bill went on to moralize:

Thick pilotis, thin pilotis, pilotis of whimsical shapes lacking any structural rhyme or reason, disposed all over the place; also walls entirely of reinforced concrete pointlessly confused with the columns, cutting up and destroying all form and purpose. It is the most gigantic disorder I have ever seen on a job. One is baffled to account for such barbarism as this in a country where there is a CIAM group, a country in which international congresses on modern architecture are held, where a journal like *Habitat* is published and where there is a biennial exhibition of architecture. For such works are born of a spirit devoid of all decency and of all responsibility to human needs. It is the spirit of decorativeness, something diametrically opposed to the spirit which animates architecture, which is the art of building, the social art above all others.[8]

Ernesto Rogers's article in the same journal lacked the stridency of Bill's but nevertheless also assumed a patronizing tone. To be fair, Walter Gropius and others in the same issue of *Architectural Review* were somewhat more generous. It is of relevance to note that 1954 was the same year of the aforementioned MoMA exhibit and catalogue in which Hitchcock established his selective canon of Latin American modernism. These acts, supportive or otherwise of Latin American modern architecture, nevertheless reflected the tendency of European and North American architects, historians, and critics to regard Latin American architecture in reference and subservience to their own.

Africa presented a different kind of "other" for European and North American intellectuals, particularly artists, as Giulio Carlo Argan notes:

The historical problem was not Negro sculpture but the crisis in European culture, which was forced to look outside its own circle to find value models. . . . [Picasso] realized that the value of Negro art lay in a unity, an integrity, a formal absoluteness of which Western art is ignorant because its concept of the world is according to ancient tradition, dualist: matter and spirit, particular and universal, things and space.[9]

African culture was never to have an influence in architecture as it did in European art in the 1920s and 1930s. Nevertheless, propelled by the reasons cited by Argan, and intrigued by the articles of Marcel Griaule on Dogon culture in the surrealist journal *Minotaure*, Aldo van Eyck undertook a series of journeys into central Africa.[10] Out of these trips he developed an interest in anthropology and indigenous dwelling forms, from which he would draw in the creation of the cellular plan for the Childrens' Home in Amsterdam (1955-60). This can be cited only as a parallel interest and not a precedent to Porro's investigations which take a different route. Nevertheless, it is important to note the overlapping dates and interests.

Cuban culture, unlike Dutch, is deeply imbued with African influence. Gerardo Mosquera points out that unlike European artists, Wifredo Lam's incorporation of African culture in his art is an act from within and not from without, as with Pablo Picasso, et al. Moreover, Mosquera notes that "there is the natural way in which mythological thought operates in the Caribbean within the modern conscience, without any contradiction."[11] Within this intellectual framework, Ricardo Porro's interpretation and editing of the Afro-Cuban experience makes perfect sense, if we accept that it is an act of interpretation and editing—just as Lam's work is a result of interpretation and editing. Vittorio Garatti and Roberto Gottardi do not claim any conscious Afro-centric impulses in their work. But Garatti does speak of the formal influence the paintings of Lam had on his architecture at Cubanacán. Gottardi's plan for the School of Dramatic Arts, with its anthropomorphic form and cellular disposition, as well as a somewhat anthropological attitude toward program, bears greater resemblance to Dogon form than van Eyck's school, though such resemblance may be only coincidental.

By seeking to oppose or transform the rationalist tendency of modern architecture, as discussed in the preceding examples, something interesting happened. Other modernisms demonstrated an ability to embrace a multitude of diverse ideas. Other modernisms provided inclusive environments where diverse cultural and technological impulses could cohabit and interact, responding to diverse human conditions. The National Art Schools, while indeed very unique examples of formal expression, nevertheless form part of this "other" tradition.

NOTES

1. Zehra Kuz, *Autochthone Architektur in Tirol*, (Vienna: Herausgeber und Ausstellungskomitee, 1992), 9.

2. Kenneth Frampton, *Modern Architecture, A Critical History*, (London: Thames and Hudson, 1992), 332. The chapter "Critical Regionalism: Modern Architecture and Cultural Identity," is highly instructive for its description and analysis of issues of identity and regionalism.

3. Ernesto Rogers, "Le preesistenze ambientali e i termi practici contemporanei," *Casabella-Continuitá* 204 (February-March 1955): 3–6; reprinted in Joan Ockman, *Architecture Culture 1943–1968* (New York: Columbia Books of Architecture/Rizzoli, 1993), 201.

4. Harwell Hamilton Harris, *Regional and Nationalism*, quoted in Kenneth Frampton, *Modern Architecture, A Critical History* (London: Thames and Hudson, 1992), 320. Frampton writes, "No-one has perhaps expressed the idea of a Critical Regionalism more forcefully than Harris . . . ."

5. John A. Loomis, "The Architecture of Walter Betancourt's Quiet Revolution," *Progressive Architecture* (April 1995): 41–44.

6. Joan Ockman, *Architecture Culture 1943–1968* (New York: Columbia Books of Architecture/Rizzoli, 1993), 347.

7. Max Bill, "Report on Brazil," *Architectural Review* (October 1954): 238.

8. Ibid., 238-39.

9. Giulio Carlo Argan, *Modern Art 170/1970* (Florence: 1979), 512.

10. Note that it was also the surrealists who organized one of the first exhibitions of Latin American architecture in Paris in 1938.

11. Gerardo Mosqera, "Modernism from Afro-America: Wifredo Lam," *Beyond the Fantastic, Contemporary Art Criticism from Latin America* (London: Institute of International Visual Arts, 1995), 129.

The new architecture, for the mere fact of

being in the service of the people, must not be

a purely utilitarian art, without aesthetic or

emotional purpose . . . If architectonic

construction cannot be lifted above mere

mechanical constructions, I would say it is

worthless to think of studying architecture.

Joaquín Weiss y Sánchez

SIX

Road to Rehabilitation

In 1982 a group of young architects who were critical of the way architecture was taught and practiced in Cuba began meeting informally. In 1988 they were given official status as a part of the Asociación Hermanos Saíz,[1] a young artists organization under the auspices of the Ministry of Culture. The 1980s in Cuba were a period that produced highly polemical, even protest, art. The Ministry of Culture had a higher tolerance for discord than the Ministry of Construction, and it was for this reason that young architects sought to associate themselves there and join the polemical activities of the so-called "Generation of the Eighties."[2] High on their agenda was the restoration of the National Art Schools to Cuba's architectural heritage. This was not necessarily a safe position to take at this time, yet the Ministry of Culture allowed them a certain latitude. In 1991 they organized a provocative exhibit entitled *Arquitectura Joven* that was presented as part of the Fourth Havana Bienal. Prominent in the exhibition was a piece by Rosendo Mesías, entitled *Revolución es Construir. . . Arquitectura.* It was a photomontage mural featuring the stark Orwellian facade of the Ministry of Construction, crumbling away (not unlike the recent Berlin Wall) to reveal emerging through the cracks—the National Art Schools.

This image was more than just a provocative gesture: the authority of MICONS had been eroding or at least changing. The optimistic plans for centrally planned, standardized construction had failed to sufficiently resolve the country's building needs, especially housing. By the early 1970s an alternative system of "microbrigades," was introduced by MICONS itself. This system relied on volunteer construction workers utilizing more conventional construction techniques to augment the lagging efforts by MICONS professionals. In 1983 architects and engineers were reorganized once again, this time into the Cuban National Union of Architects and Engineers (UNAICC). However, this time the architects were granted an entity of their own within the structure of UNAICC. This was the reconstituted Colegio de Arquitectos, a symbolic though important recognition of

OPPOSITE: *View through* paseo arquitectónico, *School of Music*
(HAZEL HANKIN)

Rosendo Mesías, Revolución es Construir. . . Arquitectura, *(1991)*
(COLLECTION OF THE ARTIST)

architecture's independent professional identity. By the late 1980s architects increasingly started to work directly for individual ministries or government organizations, indicating that a de facto process of decentralization was underway. Within this changing scenario, the physical and political rehabilitation of the National Art Schools appeared possible, though it would be a slow and, to-date, incomplete process.

Other positive events contributed to the efforts of the young architects in Hermanos Saíz. In 1986 Roberto Gottardi, who has remained in Cuba, was asked by the Instituto Superior de Arte to submit a proposal for the completion of the School of Dramatic Arts and renovation of the other schools. These plans were soon shelved and never acted upon. In 1989 a small in-house exhibit at the architecture school of the CUJAE organized by Elmer López,[3] featured some images of the National Art Schools along with other works of Cuban architecture. This seemingly unremarkable act, within this modest little exhibit—which took place the same year the Berlin Wall came down—was a gesture resonant with meaning in a faculty that had been for the most part hostile to the schools. In 1993 Sergio Baroni published "Report from Havana," in *Zodiac* 8, a thoughtful and favorable account of all five schools and their architects. He carefully avoided, however, a discussion of the ideological issues and controversy that marked their history.[4] Also in 1993, Roberto Segre published a much less critical article than any of his previous writings on the schools.[5] In 1994 the School of Plastic Arts—whose staff, along with that of the School of Modern Dance, has taken moderate care of its facilities—hosted a part of the Havana International Bienal within its exhibit space. Walls were painted, and things generally spruced up and put in good order for the first large group of international visitors since the UIA congress of 1963.

ABOVE: *School of Ballet. The foyer, 1996* (JOSÉ ALBERTO FIGUEROA)
BELOW: *School of Ballet, pavillion with* medio puntos, *1996* (JOSÉ ALBERTO FIGUEROA)

Road to Rehabilitation

ABOVE: *School of Music. Classroom, 1997* (HAZEL HANKIN)
BELOW: *School of Music. Classroom with detail of built-in seating, 1997* (JOHN A. LOOMIS)

School of Music. The paseo arquitectónico *at entry, 1994* (HAZEL HANKIN)

In April 1995 upon another initiative by Hermanos Saíz, an exhibition was organized showing the work of North American photographer, Hazel Hankin, who had extensively documented the National Art Schools in their various states of abandon and use. The exhibition was held in the gallery of the UNAICC. It was of no small significance that the works of Porro, Gottardi, and Garatti should be celebrated within the walls of this official organization which had not been known for being supportive of the schools. Despite the positive reception of the exhibit, mixed messages were presented in the accompanying catalog by architectural historian Eliana Cárdenas. While granting the schools faint praise, she advanced no real new analysis, other than to echo some of the critique found in Segre's earlier works. For example:

> . . . the National Art Schools will not be considered as a symbol of the architecture of the Revolution; they will be appreciated as representations of a persistence of a concept of an architecture that pertains to the past, of the individual genius, of an expensive architecture, completed and delayed in its execution.[6]

Cárdenas went on to chide the young architects "who have put [the schools] on a podium and pay them blind respect."[7] This simultaneous celebration and criticism of the schools is symptomatic of an ideological schizophrenia that is slowly coming to a resolution.

Later in 1995 the art schools were nominated for national landmark status along with other projects that represented the architecture of the Revolution: the CUJAE, schools by Josefina Rebellón, and Martyrs' Park by Emilio Escobar Loret de Mola and Mario Coyula Cowley. None of the projects nominated received landmark designation, not for political reasons, but because the conservative inclinations of the national board considered all of the projects too recent to be considered "historic," and therefore could not be considered landmarks.

The symbolic resonance of the National Art Schools, so important to the young architects, still makes a number of the older *apparat* uncomfortable.[8] Some of them insist in maintaining earlier positions, such as the "inappropriateness" of the schools, especially when having to show them to foreign visitors.[9] Much of the Cuban architectural establishment today accepts the architectural value of the schools with a mixture of reluctance and embarrassment. That the schools have become so abused and deteriorated, as especially evidenced in the Ballet school, is not something about which this establishment can take much pride. This accounts in part for much of the hesitant attitude toward their rehabilitation. In 1996, upon the initiative of Cuban cultural officials, two New York architects, Norma Barbacci and Ricardo Zurita, prepared nomination papers on behalf of the schools for the World Monuments Watch. An impressive dossier was assembled with letters of support from a distinguished group of international architects and historians. But when it was time for a Cuban official to sign off, none of the previously supportive advocates in Cuba would come forth to assume responsibility. Even though the World Monuments Fund generously extended the deadline in their case, eventually the nomination of the schools had to be dropped. Despite this setback, within Cuba the schools were officially designated as a "protected zone" in 1997, making them now eligible for future designation as landmarks, even though this status had been denied in 1995. Also in 1997, the National Conservation Institute (CENCREM) sponsored the preparation of a field report by architect Ernesto Jiménez García to establish the extent of the deterioration of the schools and to propose steps toward stablizing their condition. This report outlined an estimate of two million dollars for the complete restoration of the schools. However, the only immediate plans for restoration, which have been contracted to CENCREM, are for waterproofing the cupolas of the four dance pavilions of the School of Modern Dance.[10] With Cuba's more recent tentative ventures into state capitalism, there has been mention in the notoriously active rumor mill, *la bola*, of plans to restore the country club's golf course for tourists—and to turn the schools into restaurants, bars and other facilities for the leisure activities of dollar-paying foreigners. The political as well as physical rehabilitation of the National Art Schools is far from a linear process.

As for the architects, they all have continued on in productive careers. Roberto Gottardi continues to live, practice, and teach architecture in Cuba. Among his more important achievements is the Agricultural Center (1968) in Menocal. Vittorio Garatti is credited with the Escuela André Voisin in Güines (1962) and the Cuba Pavilion for Montreal's Expo '67 (with Sergio Baroni and Hugo D'Acosta, 1966-67), as well as the Master Plan for Havana (with Max Vaquero, Jean Pierre Garnier, and Eusebio Azcue, 1968-70) prior to his forced departure. He today suspects that his expulsion might have been a result of a CIA disinformation campaign within Cuba designed to alienate foreign professionals from their Cuban counterparts. Garatti maintains a successful practice in Milan as evidenced by his renovation of the Grand Hotel Galia (1990–91) and other projects. In Paris, Ricardo Porro has achieved a number of significant projects, especially in more recent years, such as the College Elsa Triollet (1990) in Saint Denis, and the College Fabien (1993) in Montrueil. It is ironic that these and most of Porro's other projects, schools, housing, and social services, are all found in the Communist municipalities surrounding Paris. "I have always been a social architect," Porro declares. "I build for the children of workers and immigrants." His work continues to operate in a highly figurative and symbolic venue, very much contrary to the state modernism of the Mitterand and post-Mitterand regimes. He is also active as a painter and sculptor.

For all practical purposes, the architects can be considered "rehabilitated" politically, even though their projects remain quite the opposite physically. Vittorio Garatti first returned to Cuba in June 1988 for a personal visit. He received a written welcome from Carlos Rafael Rodríguez acknowledging his contributions to the country. Garatti returned again in June 1997 and lectured at the Colegio de Arquitectos. His talk was well received and a subject of discussion among architects for months afterward. Ricardo Porro's return in March 1996 marked an important turning point for the reappreciation of the art schools, though his trip was initially clouded with mixed messages. His invitation, sponsored by old friends through the now reconstituted Colegio de Arquitectos, was considered so controversial that it had to be cleared by the Central Committee of the Cuban Communist Party. It was originally agreed that Porro would give five public lectures. However, officials responsible became apprehensive as the date for his arrival neared and decided that his lectures would be "by invitation only." Porro, upon hearing this, threatened to cancel his trip, causing the Colegio no small amount of embarrassment, upon which officials retracted and reaffirmed that the lectures would be public. Unknown to himself, Porro had become a bit of a mythic, if not cult figure, especially among the young architecture students in Cuba. He resembled the Pied Piper, followed by a flock of curious young students as he toured the School of Plastic Arts and the School of Modern Dance, where he was presented with a performance in his honor. His lectures were attended by standing-room-only audiences and were heralded as "one of the most important cultural events of recent years" in *Revolución y Cultura*, which also published an extensive interview with him by María Elena Martin Zequeira.[11] Following this event, Roberto Segre published a new essay on Cuban architecture in which he portrayed the art schools in a favorable light, for the first time absent of any criticism whatsoever.[12] However, not everyone welcomed Porro. Officials of the Union of Writers and Artists (UNEAC) adamantly denied any opportunity for him to lecture in their halls. Porro returned again in January 1997 at the invitation of Selma Díaz, now director of Habitat Cuba. She had arranged for him to conduct a three-week charrette with a group of architecture students. He also met with Ministry of Tourism officials regarding a possible hotel project at Playa Varadero. And, this time, he was invited to give a lecture at UNEAC. He also returned in May 1998 to participate in a round-table discussion on Cuban architecture of the 1950s. Later in 1998, issue 377 of *Arquitectura Cuba* was dedicated to Porro and his work. The importance of this official recognition cannot be underestimated. And it was an achievement not without struggle on the part of the journal's director and editors. The subsequent issue 378 was dedicated to Roberto Gottardi and his work.

NOTES

1. The Saíz brothers, for whom the organization is named, were two young, revolutionary poets killed during the armed struggle. Some of the members of the association were Emma Alvarez Tabío, Teresa Ayuso, Francisco Bedoya, Daniel Bejerano, Rafael Fornés, Rosendo Mesías, Juan Luis Morales Menocal, Eduardo Luis Rodríguez and Patricia Rodríguez Alomá.

2. It should be noted that while the National Art Schools themselves have been much neglected, arts education in Cuba has not. For a country with limited economic resources, Cuba has nevertheless made arts education a priority, with undeniably impressive results. The educational system has produced an abundance of talented and well-prepared visual artists, musicians, and dancers. However, given the limited professional opportunities in Cuba during the late 1980s and early 1990s, many of these artists chose to seek their fortunes abroad after completing their educations and achieving initial successes in Cuba. Today, with a somewhat improved economy, the tendency is to remain, while exhibiting and performing internationally. For a comprehensive survey of Cuban visual artists, see Adolfo V. Nodal, Cristina Vives Gutiérrez, José Veigas, Valia Garzon, Dannys Deoca, *Memoria: Cuban Art of the Twentieth Century* (Sydney: Craftsman House Press, 1999).

3. López was a dedicated and popular faculty member, very integrated into the Revolution, who later inexplicably disappeared.

4. Baroni, Sergio. "Report from Havana," *Zodiac 8, International Review of Architecture*, (1993): 160-183.

5. Roberto Segre, "Tres décadas de arquitectura cubana: La herencia histórica y el mito de lo nuevo," *Arquitectura Antillana del siglo XX*, Universidad Autónoma Metropolitana-Unidad Xochimilco, (Mexico City, 1993).

6. Eliana Cardenas, "Las Escuelas Nacionales de Arte, un pretexto para continuar la polemica," *Hazel Hankin Fotografias—Abril 1995* (Havana: Colegio de Arquitectos UNAICC, 1995), 8.

7. Ibid.

8. It should be noted that some of the *apparat* who had been uninvolved in the power struggle waged by MICONS, never subscribed to the ideologically framed attacks against the art schools. One such official of important stature was Carlos Rafael Rodríquez, Cuba's late Vice President who wrote approvingly of the schools in 1967 (see quote pp 20–21, herein).

9. See, for example quotes from Peter Noever, ed., *The Havana Project—Architecture Again.* (New York: Prestel, 1996). "The architects [of the Art Schools] were proceeding with an architecture of the intelligentsia, based on care. But clearly with no audience. In fact, one senses the radicalness of a lack of audience."—Thom Mayne p. 30. ". . . To make it clear: the Art Schools are not revolutionary. They are self-concentrated, personal statements."—Wolf Prix, p. 31, and ". . . It is a personal statement with a lot of qualities, but its aesthetics were not suitable for the context in which it arose."—Wolf Prix p. 34. These comments were clearly influenced by the commentary of these distinguished visitors' Cuban guides.

10. Ernesto Jiménez García, *La Escuela Nacional de Artes (Información General)* (Havana: CEN-CREM, 1997).

11. María Elena Martin Zequeria, "Arquitectura: Hallar el Marco Poético," interview with Ricardo Porro, *Revolución y Cultura* 5 (1996): 44–51.

12. R. Segre, "La Habana siglo XX: espacio dilatado y tiempo contraído," *Ciudad y Territorio, Estudios Territoriales*, XXVIII (110), 1996.

AFTERWORD

History will absolve me.

Fidel Castro

The National Art Schools were conceived from a point of view which embraced the rich diversity of Cuban culture. This cultural position was then given form through the tectonic discipline of the Catalan vault, which provided opportunities for free organic expression in the process of creating an architectural *cubanidad*. As ideology assumed a more absolutist character in revolutionary Cuba, the "official" point of view that emerged for architecture was one where the tectonic discipline, in this case predicated on functionalist industrialized systems, became the end instead of the means toward architectural expression for much of Cuban architecture. For this accepted form of architecture, *cubanidad* would emerge naturally from the technical process with no real formal guidance from the architect. History has now proved this latter approach to be a far more "idealist" position than that of the architects for the National Art Schools, though idealism is one of the fundamental criticisms they endured.

The National Art Schools now stand as an artifact representing a particular vision of the Cuban Revolution. This vision was inherently humanist and pluralist, and could be concretized through craft traditions. It regarded revolution as a truly liberating experience embracing race, cultural diversity, tropical beauty, spontaneity, and sensuality integrated with political consciousness. It was a vision that accepted the subjective and irrational side of reality, a vision that looked to local history as a means of conceiving a socialist future. What could more validate this vision than the almost carnevalesque inversion of an elitist country club into a proletarian experimental arts school? Who could deny that this was a very appealing vision?

However, the prevailing socialist vision required obedience, centralized authority, communal discipline, controlled sexuality (no homosexuality) and an internationalist orientation. This vision could only be concretized in industrialized processes definitive of a modern material socialist culture and derived from the rationalist and functionalist traditions. While the ultimate dominance of this second vision had much to do with the spon-

OPPOSITE: *Congero, School of Modern Dance*
(HAZEL HANKIN)

sorship of the Soviet Union, the struggle between the two visions also represented the subjective rivalries among ambitious individuals competing for prominence in a profession that was in the process of redefinition in order to position itself in the new social order. As the state shifted its patronage from the first vision to the second, it was inevitable that the schools would be left behind as artifacts.

The drama of the National Art Schools did not take place in any of the main arenas of twentieth century architecture. The fact that it took place on the margin is one of the reasons that they are not well known. But it is also their existence on the margin that accounts for their creativity and resistance to dominant cultural forces. The National Art Schools were geographically marginal, located in a small underdeveloped country ninety miles from the U.S. They were geopolitically marginal, that country having just declared itself socialist and Marxist-Leninist. Within that country's capital city they also were marginal, located far from the urban center on its suburban outskirts. Most importantly though, they were marginal in terms of architectural design, having rejected existing forms of linguistic expression in favor of an attempt to create a radical, formal alternative to contemporary architectural language, seeking to engage the specific environmental, political, and utopian ethos of a new emerging culture.

Despite their partial disappearance in the overgrown vegetation of Cubanacán, the National Art Schools stand today, after more than thirty years, as the most memorable architectural works of the Cuban Revolution and its most genuine architectural expression of *cubanidad*.

History will absolve the National Art Schools.

EPILOGUE

In 1999 a most memorable encounter happened at the close of a lecture based on *Revolution of Forms*, which I had given to a group of architects and architectural educators gathered in Minneapolis for the annual Association of Collegiate Schools of Architecture conference. Shawn Rickenbacker, then a young assistant professor at Ohio State University, approached me very animatedly and said, "Now I understand. Everything my grandfather told me was true!"

Shawn recounted that his "grandfather" was actually his step-grandfather, whom his grandmother had married after she was widowed and before Shawn was born. This grandfather—Cuban and a mason—was welcomed into her warm African American extended family in the Bronx. Shawn remembered him as a gregarious, larger-than-life character, a teller of tall tales. He was loved by all, but his stories always needed to be taken with a grain of salt. Among the stories he told Shawn was one about building a group of art schools in Havana shortly after the Revolution. The structures, of brick and tile and of forms and spaces that curved and flowed, had been inspired by Afro-Cuban culture and constructed as architecture had never been before. Shawn's grandfather considered the schools his greatest achievement as a master mason, and, as in all of his stories, he himself played an instrumental role. Shawn, who had a hard time believing that such buildings really existed, filed the story away with his grandfather's other tall tales. That is, until the day of the lecture.

This was a wonderful, unexpected consequence of having written about the National Art Schools in *Revolution of Forms*. But there were also other wonderful surprises. Shortly after the publication of the book, I received a letter from Brother Stephen Galban of Mount Saviour Monastery in New York, complimenting the book and naming the "unidentified architect" in the caption of the bottom photograph on page six as Enrique Govantes, now a member of that Benedictine community. At a lecture in 2000 at Washington State University, Seattle, a man came up to me and emotionally thanked me for mentioning the artist Tomás Oliva in the book. The man was Tomás Oliva Jr.

Carlos Batista, son of architect Eugenio Batista, Cuba's most important early modernist and theoretician, approached me after another talk—I cannot remember where—and spoke with me about his father and family. At another speaking event, I met Carlos's sister (Eugenio Batista's daughter). And after a lecture at The Getty Center in 2004, the granddaughter of architect Welton Becket, who had several major projects in Havana during the 1950s, introduced herself to me.

The story of the art schools is a very compelling one and goes far beyond conventional architectural history. It embraces the age-old human desire for a better world and reveals the tragic human processes that impede the pursuit of utopia—although hope can never be fully banished. It moves me to have discovered how many people, Cuban and non-Cuban alike, feel a connection to the story and also to know that the schools have made a lasting impact on architectural, as well as Cuban, history.

I met Felipe Dulzaides, a Cuban artist, at an art opening in San Francisco in 1999. He had studied at the National Art Schools for many years and had often marveled at the beauty of the architecture there—especially the magic realist aura evoked by the group of buildings. He had been unaware of their origins until he came upon *Revolution of Forms* in the United States. His artistic response to the story came later that year in the form of a video-documented performance-art piece called *Next Time it Rains the Water Will Run*, in which he lovingly cleans out the watercourses of the abandoned School of Ballet. The channels, which had filled up over the years with leaves and debris, had originally been designed by Garrati to not only carry away rainwater but to create an aqueous musical dance, with the water descending, racing and leaping from level to level around the school, in search of a place to rest—a pool at the end of the course. As the water runs, the video also conveys ambient sounds resonating in the acoustic volumes of the Catalan vaults as abstract music within the ruins. The performance brought tears to Garatti's eyes when he saw the video in Milan.

The story of the National Art Schools lingered with Dulzaides. The artistic yearning and search for utopia resonated with this Cuban, who had grown up in Cuba during the Revolution. He befriended Gottardi, and together they explored and represented Gottardi's artistic process in designing the School of Dramatic Arts—as well as the relationship between this process and the pursuit of utopia—in a performance/installation in 2004 for the Proyecto Invitación in Havana, which was followed by a more extensive, and highly acclaimed, installation titled *Utopía posible* at the Gwangju Biennial (South Korea) in 2008 and the Havana Biennial in 2009. This endeavor also evolved into a documentary video titled *Utopía posible*—a series of penetrating, and sometimes disquieting, interviews with Gottardi about his artistic quest for meaning during his years in Revolutionary Cuba.

Non-Cubans have also been inspired by the universal nature of the story of the National Art Schools. Alysa Nahmias was so moved by the schools she saw during her study abroad experience as an undergraduate at New York University in Cuba that she began working on a documentary film about the schools in 2001. It started as a student project but then became a decade-long undertaking. The film (with the working title *Unfinished Spaces*) is a visually rich production, with dazzling cinematography by Ben Murray, that truly captures the magic of the spaces. Nahmias's compelling interviews with the architects and others involved in their story, dig deeply into the history of the schools. The film is expected to premiere at Sundance Film Festival in 2011.

Filmmaker Charles Koppelman was also inspired by *Revolution of Forms* and sought a medium that would embrace all of the arts: visual arts, music, dance, and theater. His vision was of an opera for which he is both librettist and producer. Anthony Davis and Dafnis Prieto are composing the music, and Robert Wilson is directing the production. Koppelman saw that this particular journey—a universal human quest to create a better world—played itself out in a heroic and classic literary arc of passion, love, betrayal, despair, and ultimately hope. It is in production to become a multilingual opera in five acts. The date for the premier is yet to be announced.

It is a wonderful, unintended consequence that the story told in *Revolution of Forms* has been given additional lives through these other narratives. It is apparent that when it comes to Havana's National Art Schools, *somos una familia muy grande.*

DOCUMENTS

Ricardo Porro, "El Sentido de la Tradición,"
Nuestro Tiempo 16, año IV (1957).

Architecture today has two goals. The first is to have significant social purpose. With sociologists and economists planning new forms of social organization that are in accordance with our times, it is logical that the architect in
his art will try to express the new meaning of these conditions. The second
goal is to ensure that architecture, instead of being international, is part of a
local tradition.

The realization of the first proposition is impossible for the moment in most
countries, among them Cuba, given our social conditions. The Cuban architect, when involved in urban planning, works for an investor who desires
immediate profits with the sale of individual lots and he wants nothing to do
with traditional models for fear of a bad investment. If contemporary Cuban
architects involve themselves with the problem of the community, our projects remain on paper, with no immediate hopes of realization.

There is only left to us in these times the attempt to achieve the second goal.
It is to ensure that the architecture that is made in Cuba is Cuban, that it
continues our tradition.

The word "tradition" requires definition. Tradition does not mean the faithful
copying of the past; the result would be archaeology, not architecture. This
naturally would destroy the artistic creation and by that token, tradition. Neither does it mean to faithfully copy superficial decorative details; this would
be falsehood. The result would be the pseudo-colonial houses of Miramar or
the eclectic ones of El Vedado.

Tradition is not contrary to creation. Artistic tradition is the result in art of the
way of life of a people who have their own customs and habits. It is the
thoughtful incarnation of their mentality. That is to say that art has to express
the particular culture of a certain people who live in a certain place. It is the
expression of a reciprocal action between man and the place in which he
develops, the sum of his experiences, the expression of the spiritual characteristics common to a people. . . .

The indigenous races were exterminated at the beginning of colonization,
and from them we have inherited almost nothing from the cultural point of

view. We are a product of the Spaniard, above all the Spaniard of the southern part of the peninsula, and of the black African. From here comes forth our character. The mixture of the severe and intense Spaniard with the black African has produced, in our midst, warm and easy going, a man of extreme sensuality.

Fidel Castro Ruz, "Palabras a los intelectuales," 30 June 1961, as quoted in "La más hermosa academia de artes de todo el mundo," *Noticias de Hoy* (4 May 1963)

The National Academy of Art has just begun to be built, apart from the National Academy of Manual Arts. For certain, Cuba will count as having the most beautiful academy of arts in the whole world. Why? Because this academy is situated in one of most beautiful residential developments in the world, where the most wealthy of Cuba's bourgeoisie lived: in the best estate of the most ostentatious and the most luxurious and the most vulgar bourgeoisie, this said in passing, because in none of these houses was there lacking a bar, their inhabitants had no worries except for the problems of their little social world. They lived in an incredibly luxurious manner and it is worth it to take a stroll over there to see how these people lived; but there is no way they could have known what an extraordinary academy of art is being constructed and this is what will remain of what they made, because the students are going to live in the houses that were the residences of millionaires. They will not live cloistered; they will live as if at home and they will attend the classes in the Academy; the Academy is going to be situated in the middle of the country club, where a group of architects—artists, have designed the constructions they are going to realize. They have just started, and they have the commitment to complete them by this December. We now have three thousand board feet of mahogany. The schools of music, dance, ballet, theater and plastic arts will be in the middle of the golf course, in a natural environment that is a dream. There will be the Academy of Art, with sixty residences, situated around it, with the clubhouse at one side, which has dining rooms, meeting rooms, swimming pool and also an apartment for visitors, where foreign professors who come to help us can lodge. This academy will have the capacity for three thousand students, that is to say three thousand students on scholarship, and with the hope to commence in the next term.

Rafael López Rangel, *Arquitectura y Subdesarrollo en América Latina*
(Puebla: Universidad Autónoma de Puebla, 1975).

It appears evident that the architectonic language of the Art Schools does not
obey the "semantic field" of the Revolution, because in reality the structuring
of its forms are organized in accordance with individualistic, arbitrary, conceptual lines not organically incorporated and coparticipant in the definition
of the character and type of revolutionary process. Because of this, no matter
how interesting and attractive are the undulations of the volumes of the
schools by the architects Ricardo Porro, Vittorio Garatti and Roberto Gottardi;
no matter how undeniably masterful is the use of brick and the construction
of the vaults; no matter how well or carefully arranged (the spatial disposition) are the masses in the magnificent place in which they are situated (the
exclusive and aristocratic ex-jockey club); no matter how ably executed are
the details in respect to the complex—the works contain a meaning incoher-
ent with the values of the Revolution. The formalist conception that assumes
the attributes of sensuality-sexuality as the "constant of the Cuban tempera-
ment," along with the formal exuberance of the tropicalism and the African-
ism, are they not more identified with the values of the dominant classes in
the prerevolutionary period? In effect, does not this image of a Cuba of this
type correspond more to the idea of the "Isla del Turismo y del Placer," of
Cuban-folk, or those tropical curios that so please the Yankees? It is clear
enough that they are more identified with these values than with the true
ethos of the first socialist society of Latin America. Moreover, as has been
pointed out by others (Segre), in these works it is shown that function has
been sacrificed on the gallows of formal preconception.

Roberto Segre, *La Arquitectura de la Revolución Cubana*
(Montevideo: Facultad de Arquitectura Universidad de la Republica, 1968).

The National Art Schools form the most polemical and spectacular complex realized by the Revolution: widely disseminated at an international level, considered by some as the genuine expression of revolutionary architecture, they are at the same time repudiated, classified within a series of errors committed in this so called "romantic" period. . . .

Even though the constructive system is a homogenizing element for the complex, each building constitutes a unique entity, separate from the rest, not realizing the creation of a "city of the arts" legible at an urban scale and not permitting the collective use of common functional elements. The team of architects maintained their individualism, monumentalizing each solution, transcending functionalist values to become unique symbols of the historic moment. A moment that recovers certain national "constants": the presence of the "baroque" in Cuban culture, the spatial transparencies and closed patios of colonial architecture. Is it possible to discuss whether historic heritage must project itself within the revolutionary process by means of the glorification of traditional materials and closed monumental forms. In the first place, it is impossible to realize in a short time, within the context of underdevelopment, works of such breadth. In the second place, a particular situation—the scarcity of materials brought on by the economic blockade—can define only one stage of the construction, surmountable by the appropriate development of the country. If the project is conceived as an open form, transformable, additive, and functional, the work does not live for just one historic moment, but in the process, adapting itself to different alternatives, in the progressive use of the forms. If instead it is a closed system, limited by its formal virtuosity produced by craft methods, the work has value only as a complete and finished form: value is not obtained as has happened through the abandonment and ruin of the construction.

The Revolution is a collective work, whose end is the creation of a new society. It constitutes a dynamic process, vigorous, impossible to crystallize in formal symbols that do not coincide with the functional use intended for the community, inherent to the rigor imposed by the scarcity of available resources, a transitory condition of underdevelopment. For the other part, none of the acts of the people are grandiloquent and studied, but on the contrary, they always conserve the freshness of spontaneity. The monumental implies authoritarianism, order derived from above to below in pyramid fashion; therefore, can monumentality be expressive of a the Cuban political process, based in the dialogue and constant integration between the leaders and the masses? Therefore, can the space of the artist be monumentalized? Can he exile himself from the bosom of society, submerged in Arcadia; can he produce a creative act that is not born from real daily life experience of the revolutionary process? Even though the National Art Schools constitute the most intense aesthetic and spatial experience realized by the modern Cuban architecture, their forms do not coincide with the new contents; the formal exuberance is not accompanied by the scientific rigor necessary to respond efficiently to the functional needs. The thirteen million pesos invested in this complex, condition the effectiveness of an architecture that above all must be the real representation of the material and spiritual necessities of society, and not the product of a particularized, problematic interpretation carried over from the cultural background of the designer. Within such limits, hypotheses for the future are converted into utopia; into fiction. Reality is materially conditioned.

Hugo Consuegra, "Las Escuelas Nacionales de Arte,"
Aquitectura Cuba 334 (1965): 14–21.

Cuba, a small underdeveloped country, in the most difficult moment of its history, when in order to survive it must stand up to the colossal North American, in the midst of an economic blockade and armed acts of aggression, it permits itself the luxury of building—at a cost of more than thirteen million pesos—schools of art of such scope that are not seen in even London, Paris, New York or Rome.

What sense could this have? How does one explain it? Five schools of art (Ballet, Dramatic Arts, Modern Dance, Plastic Arts and Music) with five separate theaters, five libraries, and five cafeterias, among other economic excesses, how can the common use of these services be thought of? Is this not out of scale? How can one justify the state of mind that moves such an initiative? One could respond: What is one to think of a small underdeveloped country just ninety miles from the United States that declares itself the "first socialist country in America?" A small country whose economy, production and markets were entirely controlled and organically dependent upon its colossal enemy, and dares to break this dependence and live in perpetual threat. David and Goliath! Out of scale, without a doubt.

The foreigner who visits the schools of art, independently of whether he likes them of not—most often he is enthused with them—receives a sensation of excess and grandiloquence, and he naturally lends himself to criticism, above all if he is among those architects educated in the assumptions of a more direct, less spectacular architecture. But also, one may ask oneself here: is it not grandiloquent and spectacular our historic moment? A revolution that delivers for history the Second Declaration of Havana, before more than a million citizens—within a total population of six million—gathered in the public plaza. A revolution that during the so called "October Crisis," prepared to confront any risk, with complete independence, strengthening itself through its sense of moral purpose and in its willingness to sacrifice if necessary.

If Cuban culture—in any of its manifestations—aspires to reflect the Revolution, I estimate that it must do so fully aware of a certain excessiveness; meaning: freely indiscreet and shockingly realistic. We cannot be Swedes or Finns ninety miles from the United States, though we have much admiration for their architecture and though we understand well that it would give to us a measure of serenity. The National Art Schools, above and beyond the personal expression of their creators—two Italian architects and one Cuban—are the expression of this moment in revolutionary Cuba.

It has been said that they are "baroque." Ricardo Porro himself, author of the schools of Plastic Arts and Modern Dance has written: "A classical sense of space would not lend itself to this (referring to the characterization of the spaces), neither to the images that I wish to achieve. They were needing a richness of architectonic elements, fluid and varied spaces. The result was a great 'barroquismo.'" I am not totally in agreement. Of course the schools, those of Porro as well as that of Roberto Gottardi—Dramatic Arts—and those of Vittorio Garatti—Music and Ballet—are far from what could be called a classical sense of space; but I propose that in place of "baroque," a term that seems to me much more correct, "mannerist." For many reasons: the baroque is not characterized by unfolding and contorted forms, it is simply controlled by a homogenous concept; there exists a "baroque logic" within which the presence of a "totality" is expressed by the necessity for synthesis and sub- ordination: the great rhythms of the baroque. In the schools of art this does not exist; on the contrary, it is systematic, in each of their authors, that when one of these rhythms is initiated and starts growing, orchestrating itself with increasing resonance and we wait for it to culminate "in the baroque man- ner," then at precisely this point we are cast down into uncertainty as one fallen into an abyss and all sense of "development" is broken.

There is here perhaps the most profound correspondence between architec- ture and revolution. A feeling suspended between happiness and anguish; the jubilant moral sense of a people that are flourishing in the creation of their own proper national identity, free from the bonds and insults that signify for us imperialist colonialism, and on the other hand, the anguish, the perma- nent threat of destruction by this same imperialism.

In the first place, the split between the creator and his medium. It is not important whether the architects of these works are Cuban or foreign, they are, by their architectural formation and work, true "cultural aristocrats:" humanist architects, products of the whole complexity of contemporary cul- ture. It is well understood that these "aristocrats" are faithful to the Revolu- tion, they march shoulder to shoulder with the people to harvest cane and they stand guard rifle in hand, but meanwhile as architects they are alone. Their work is therefore understood in part, enjoyed only by their equals; delights of the intentions of their details; art of spatial exquisiteness, that is not even valued by all architects, except by those "exquisite architects." In front of this art, the average man reacts favorably pleased, "enchanted" it is worth saying, but without real command of his criteria, impressed by and large by the spectacle. This disproportion between the work—that is, of course, not only a spectacle—and the normal capacity to evaluate it, is pres- ent in all contemporary art; this is the case in all countries, even in those of high cultural development, but in an underdeveloped country like ours, the disproportion is truly painful. In these moments the authors of the National

Art Schools, that which they represent within our culture, and their example for the young generation of architects are the cause of a vigorous polemic in Cuba. They have become symbols, ferociously and arrogantly attacked now more than ever. The outcome of this polemic will determine for the large part the course and future of Cuban architecture. Such is its historic importance for us.

Possibly that which is most interesting for the critic is found in the common desire—in all the schools—to disintegrate the spatial unity. Disintegration that is not the multiple baroque vision, orchestrated within a whole, but the disturbing qualities of a mannerist assault on this whole, which it physically of psychically destroys. Observe how in all the schools this has been the fundamental principle. Isolated pavilions, with their independent covers in Drama, Ballet and Plastic Arts, articulating themselves according to asyncopated rhythms—unexpected rhythms, it is important to point out—give an additive vision, never total. But this desire for the disintegration of the spatial unity, that in the mentioned schools is a natural consequence of the solution for the pavilions, becomes truly surprising in the other schools.

The School of Music, an enormous continuous band—330 metres long—from the individual cubicles it goes flexing like the dormitories of Alvar Aalto at MIT in Cambridge. At first glance, what appears to us in plan is a very unitary development, but when we are expecting a continuous result, as in Bath or Crescent Park in London, we encounter a series of displacements in the design that fragment all sense of homogeneity: transversally, its fifteen metres of width are broken into two levels and covered by undulating vaults, while longitudinally the building fractures into faults that descend or rise with the terrain; each cut, moreover, is emphasized by the piling up of the sides of the eaves flowing upwards. The design of the two theaters and the plaza—still under construction—are also conceived in the same spirit. Above the powerful towers of concrete is arranged the elevated circulation, of a very poetic character, that which—towers and galleries—is the true leit-motiv of the composition; elements purely theatrical—stage, audience, vertical elements, covering—are introduced within this strong articulation of aerial elements and gardens which invade all around. It would be with great difficulty to "disintegrate" better an element so characterized as a theater.

If Garatti's solutions in the School of Music are elaborate, those of Gottardi in Dramatic Arts are truly unusual. Toward the theater, the focal point of all the functions, the different specialties of the school are grouped by sectors: sound and light, make-up, costumes, props and scenery. A very compact plan in which each locale is tied to its neighbor in angular articulations that produce a cellular web. I appears that here their individualization is impossible. Not withstanding, we observe from the model that each part, large or small, receives its own roof, in an effect that seems an "accumulation of objects of Arman, or those disturbing "wrappings" of Christo. As if this were not enough, to make more clear the fragmentation, the interior passages are—streets open to the sky! A true act of the mannerist exquisite.

The other common constant was that of creating—and I do not know if it was premeditated—a state of spatial anguish, that is of course very note-worthy. The schools of art endure a spatial hypertension. The means applied to achieve this is the sharpening of contrasts, of the dynamic angularities or the revolving surfaces. Above all there is a will to make permanent this disequilibrium, that is to say this perpetual movement. There are hardly any moments of rest; there is not any compensation of repose that establishes a harmony between the multiple and the unitary. Everything grows, becomes complicated, becomes exasperating, dissolving before a synthesis could succeed in establishing an order within our senses.

It is understood that this spatial anguish has created criticism. In the School of Plastic Arts, Porro organizes three powerful trumpet-shaped arches to form an entry; by tradition, by experience, by architectural convention—the three porticos of Christian churches—we expect that the central arch would be that which dominates the development of the composition. But it is here that, having just advanced twelve metres, the central opening vanishes and we can only continue in the lateral galleries: in addition the view through the central arch is blocked by a line of buttresses and gargoyles that turn, impeding any sense of axiality. If it is permitted, I would say that this is an "atheist" composition that denies to us the "path to the altar." The spectator is disarmed by the entrance, dazed, and his system of orientation collapses in a sensorial abyss.

Garatti gives us another node of anguish in the School of Ballet. In the area of the cafeteria, a small elliptical pool is shot at, as if it was an architectonic San Sebastián, by a series of pillars which—of course—resist any ordering toward a common focus. The result is that from no point can we grasp—"understand"—the form and dimension of the entire pool, that paradoxically is only ten meters long in its major axis. A most intense sensory frustration.

These effects of frustration are also very frequently found in the use of "incomplete forms." Here we see half vaults of arches that obstruct the spectator with their irresolution, revolving surfaces that do not complete their path and, very specially, these spatial interferences in which a formal development disturbs, molests another development, without a mutual articulation that resolves itself harmonically. Architectonic atonalism, we could say.

One of those elements that permit the critic to analyze the intentions of the architect is the form called the *paseo arquitectónico*, that is the spatial path prepared for the spectator. If we analyze the circulation of the five schools, we note the desire to avoid all definitive and immediate sense of directionality. The spectator is obliged to constantly change course; negating all axiality, and rebounding from one wall to another, confronted constantly with new views, constantly surprised with all the refinement and intellectual treachery of which these authors are capable. We are invited to move ourselves through in order to render intelligible the composition. But this intelligence of the work is only made possible through a mental recomposition—intellectual digestion—of the fragmented vision, that systematically denies us a point of view from which to synthesize the work.

Gottardi in Dramatic Arts, even though he places imaginary axes at both sides of the principal building—axes that converge toward the river and the theater created above the greenery—obliges us to abandon this axiality, which we cannot physically perceive, much less penetrate in the *calles* in order to understand a path through the great curved segments and to descend toward the nearby river, taking delight in the narrow spaces that are like canyons, interior patios open like small spatial oases, changes in elevation saved by stairs electrically broken above their axis, and finally, to make this passage more exciting, fissures that open toward the theater or toward the exterior, through which we see only fragmented slices.

Porro achieved, in our judgment, the most intense effects in his School of Modern Dance. There he obliges us to advance some fifty metres through an elegant and virile articulation of fortresslike walls and open portico, through which we turn ninety degrees and then pass through a spatial "bottleneck," opening into the interior plaza of the school. Up until this point, nothing abnormal, but observe this plaza: the traditional concept of the plaza is that of a "positive" space, meaning a space enclosed by a concavity where the void moves more or less circulating. Porro gives us a "negative" plaza; above which there open up three convex porticos that at the same time fold into themselves. Porro takes great delight in producing these folds, each pillar of the galleries occupies the place that chance has provided, creating abnormal relations and conflicts with its neighbors. The effect is of a dramatic agony, hypertense and conceptually subversive.

Another of the best correspondences between form and content is found expressed by Garatti in his School of Ballet. The *paseo arquitectónico* is here musical, intoxicating and enveloping: without any doubt, dancing. Always covered above by light vaults that go foliating, slashing the light, we are invited to bob, to turn, to slip along their surfaces. Fountains and walls whose upper borders serve as aqueducts, grow from the earth, sweetly unrolled, integrating themselves little by little in the dance of all the architectonic elements, that then having performed their role, like a life cycle, they diminish, dying and returning to the earth from which they had risen. The sweet intimacy, the genuine tropicalism, the delicacy of the details in the use of tile and brick, and the integration with the landscape whose vegetation is echoed, place this work among the most refined that have been constructed in our country.

I am optimistic in respect to the future of these works. Reality—as hard as it can be now—and hope—as fantastic as it might seem—are converging, all the time more vertiginously in revolutionary Cuba. Abundance will unfailingly come. The "disproportion" of the schools of art will diminish with time. To understand ourselves, we must remember that we are a people who buy Spanish dolls for the Epiphany during these moments of intense economic crisis. The National Art Schools, for their paradisical site and their relation to the maritime clubs—a fabulous monetary investment, dedicated for popular use—will without doubt, as Garatti points out, be the nucleus of a grand recreational lung for Havana, and its function as an intellectual center will be much more than a mere classroom.

Ricardo Porro, "Wifredo Lam,"
Unknown publication (1962): 46–48.

If there is a painter in our time and in our country whose work can be called revolutionary, that painter is Wifredo Lam. Revolution means a radical change of the established order, bringing with it an appreciation of human values.

Social painting is that which expresses the drama of man.

Lam's art has always been a violent accusation of the evils suffered by our people. It is not necessarily a painter's task to capture all the aspects of reality, translating them into visual art. Our century is rich in possibilities of expression, as proven by the diversity of tendencies in our epoch.

When choosing his subjects it became an obsession with him to give expression to those in our society who suffered most.

And Lam did not have far to go, for he was himself of the people. He returned to his childhood to live again in the world of poverty of the mestizos of Sagua la Grande (a town in Las Villas province).

That was the source of his inspiration. He created its symbols and converted them into the most poetic painting of today. He created terrible beings that are imagined only by men cut off from all sources of culture.

And so he gave the spectator a vision of the evil that only a revolution can change. Great tragedy is always present with Lam. I only know of one other painter who reacts to cruelty with such violence: Pablo Picasso. If the expression of reality by revolutionary painting is such that it can be used as an instrument to change the world, then Lam's art certainly falls in that category.

His painting is a call to men's conscience.

Wifredo Lam has always been a revolutionary—as man and as artist. Only the Revolution can do away with the evil which he depicts in his works.

Paolo Portoghesi, *Postmodern*
(New York: Rizzoli International, 1983): 137–38.

Porro personally experienced the Cuban Revolution and came out of it unin-
hibited, freed from what he had learned about architecture in school. His
friendship with Fidel Castro during the Revolution led to Porro's obtaining the
commission to build the National School of Plastic Arts in Havana, which
after fifteen years can still be considered one of the few original attempts to
found a popular language of architecture for the new needs of a socialist society. The art school—part of a program intended to attract young people to
Cuba from every part of Latin America, thus creating a center of revolutionary
training—lucidly interprets in architectural terms Afro-Cuban culture, which
had so much influence in the formation of modern popular music. It takes
inspiration from the archetypal forms of the villages of African huts and the
baroque domes of the Hispanic-American tradition. But it has a provocative
and disturbing side in the presence of an erotic symbolism immediately evident to the observer. The general layout, with its opposition of rigid and curvilinear forms, is a synthesis that has nothing mechanical or vulgar about it. It
suggests the structure of the genital organs and the dynamic of the sexual
act. The same themes appear when the complex is viewed from below: in the
relationship between the porticoed walkways and the spatial cells of the
classrooms, as well as in the key figure which drips water into a small fountain: shell, mouth, feminine figure par excellence. The architectural value of
the school is certainly not a direct consequence of this symbolic content. It
derives its value, rather, from the pure way in which content is translated into
forms, using the specific means of architecture, with Porro's confidence in
using the traditional masonry structure, filtered through the interpretive lens
of modern architecture, in the complementary and dialectical use of the rational element (in the control of structure and technology) and of the emotional
element, in the planning and linking of the images.

Sergio Baroni. "Report from Havana,"

Zodiac 8, *International Review of Architecture*, Renato Minetto, ed. (1993): 160–183.

Without entering into rhetorical discussion of whether and how individuals are shaped by the buildings they inhabit, there can be little doubt that the only response to the political decision to build the National Art Schools (ENA), motivated by the solidarity and libertarian ideologies of the time, could be an architectural project of the highest artistic and cultural standard. The idea of a single compact building to house the five faculties envisioned for the School—Theater, Dance, Ballet, Plastic Arts and Music—was quickly abandoned for planning and technical reasons in favor of a kind of garden complex of five separate buildings around the edge of the site that would leave the beautiful central open space and existing Country Club installations intact. Much was spoken and written about the ENA at the time, both in Cuba and abroad. If I go over the old ground again here, it is because the project is an unusual example of the kind of transculturation that has always been a prominent feature of the Cuban culture. It is worth considering here some of the things the architects commissioned to do the job had in common because it offers special insights into the scope and significance of what they achieved. The three architects, Ricardo Porro from Cuba, and Vittorio Garatti and Roberto Gottardi from Italy, were barely thirty at the time and still had little experience of actually building architecture. All three had been closely involved in the debate over the limitations and frustrations of the Modern Movement in Italy in the 1950s, had drawn their inspiration from Wright and Gaudí, had contributed to the furor over Ronchamp and the Torre Velasca, and had participated in the Art Nouveau revival. However, they had also been able to relate their experience to the dramatic and contradictory events of a primitive Venezuela where the talented Carlos Raúl Villanueva was even then bringing his vision of architecture to maturity. It was the grafting of this rich conceptual and imaginative inheritance into a program already original in itself, in a highly stimulating and extraordinarily (and justifiably) optimistic natural environment, that produced these exceptional works (in all senses of the word), unique achievements totally different from the general run of architecture at the time. Their effect on Cuban culture was to broaden the horizons of routine planning and design practice in the country. In addition to climatic and environmental research, the will to create, and better understanding and use of the site and nature, experimentation proceeded at an almost breathless pace with new spaces and forms deriving from a wide range of factual and metaphorical input that was reprocessed in various ways— changes of scale, exaggerated or broken rhythms, slopes and overhangs, complex or intersecting force and direction lines, fragmentation of volumes—to produce an approach that reflected the abstract geometrical linearity of a supposed rationality (which had already been both accepted and contradicted by transnational Havana itself) in favor of a realism founded on the complexity of a society bursting with contradictions. In this sense, the Schools still provide an indispensable, if controversial point of reference for future architecture in a changing society that professes to be building a world different from the homologous uniformity created by central ideologies. Much of the controversy over the ENA was misguided. It would be mistaken to see the arguments that emerged as *ante litteram* products of Postmodernism unless we decide first which of Postmodernism's many aspects they advocated or opposed. In point of fact, the right to reinstate the validity of architecture as an artistic medium based not on historical "signs" but on the expressive potential of its various elements—the wall, the arch, the dome, window and door frames—was widely asserted. It would also be mistaken to see the outcome of the project (three of the five schools have never been finished and the concept has never been repeated) as a political and cultural choice, that seemed to concern an elitist, hedonistic concept of architecture. That the Schools never entered the mainstream of Cuban architecture was due to factors which have continuously shaped the development of Cuban architecture since then, and have only very recently shown signs of changing.

One of these factors, perhaps the least important, was simply the program's loss of relevance. Once Cuba had been isolated from the outside world, the scale of the complex was considered disproportionate to the country's internal needs. Also, the lack of the skilled labor needed to cope with urgent, large-scale, building projects—it would eventually become chronic in the building industry—was beginning to make its presence felt. The ENA site held valuable reserves of manpower which it was decided could be usefully deployed for more urgent work elsewhere. Finally, a growing scarcity of essential finishing materials on the site—wood, ceramics, brick, electric and sanitary installations, etc.—made it increasingly difficult to bring the project to completion. Work virtually stopped, and the tangled web of arguments that would eventually be used to demonstrate the project's impracticability and justify abandoning it was gradually woven. This is now acknowledged to have been a grave mistake. It is becoming increasingly evident that the failure to finish the Schools was a set-back in a revival of Cuban architecture that had been having trouble in making headway since the pre-Revolutionary days. The Schools project, it is now realized, had speeded up the process considerably and had linked it to the country's new social project.

Personal Memories of the National Art Schools by the Artist as a Young Student, Ever Fonseca,
interview with the author (September 1997).

Ever Fonseca is one of Cuba's most internationally renowned painters. During the Revolution he had served with the rebel forces in the guerrilla war. Afterwards, having won a place in the School of Plastic Arts through a national art competition, he became a member of the first class of the school. These are some of his recollections of those first years of the National Art Schools as a young student.

It was 1962 and we were the first group of the school. We had come from all over the island, chosen by competition. Most of us would have otherwise never have had an opportunity to study art. I was the only student who had been in the rebel army. I was far away from home which had been in a poor farming community deep in the interior of Cuba. They were building the schools when we arrived as the first class. It was in a club that had been for the richest Cubans with wealthy mansions all around and it was being converted for our use. It was very beautiful then. There were still gardeners and we had "tias" who cooked for us, did our laundry and looked out for the mansions where we were now living. There was a kitchen in the club and a dining room where we all shared meals together. There were no shortages yet and we ate very well back then. There were many supplies. Two buses that both worked were for our use. The school organized vacations for us, paid for our trips home to visit our families. The directors were a very creative, innovative group. Our teachers were very dedicated and very experimental. We felt very privileged. So we students were very motivated. We had an almost military discipline then, very different from art students today.

We were living through an extraordinary social experiment. We were living in very intense, very creative times. I remember with great nostalgia, yes, voluntary work in the fields cutting cane. It was a lot of hard work but done with *un amor tan grande* because were creating paradise. You cannot begin to understand what were the hopes of those years. We truly believed that all could be transformed merely by our work into a utopia. I wish I could recapture for you the rapture of those times of our youth.

I remember Porro very well. *Una persona muy agradable y muy sensible.* We used to call him "Porbusier." He was very impressive. He had a fire in him to realize these schools and we were all very attracted by his enthusiasm. He gave classes to us too in the history of architecture, painting, and of architecture as a form of art. He would talk to us about the importance of not abandoning our roots, about the idiosyncrasies of our mixed race, about sensuality, about the curved line and the undulating plane which is the essence of Africa in us, of terra cotta which is the color of our skin.

I do not really know about the criticisms, the internal struggles. We were just young students then and did not know all that was going on. Some said the schools were not functional. Well some things were not finished. The acoustical work was not finished. Certain elements to soften the echo in the round studios were planned for but not completed. But for me the schools were functional for many reasons. The functional can be organic and aesthetic. Many do not understand this. Culturally the schools were very functional, very good for the spirit, providing a place of meditation for the students. I loved studying there in the wonderful spaces with the wonderful light. You had the sense of being alone when walking along the curved paths There was the magic of being there walking along at six in the evening in the *gran silencio.*

In those days when visitors came to Havana, first they were taken to the Plaza de la Revolución then to the Escuelas Nacionales de Arte. The art schools are really the only example we have of a revolutionary architecture.

CHRONOLOGY

SELECTED CHRONOLOGICAL EVENTS

1925	Nov. 3	**Ricardo Porro Hidalgo is born**.
		Partido Socialista Popular (PSP, Cuban Communist Party) is founded.
1926	Aug. 13	Fidel Castro Ruz is born.
1927	Jan. 30	**Roberto Gottardi is born**.
	Apr. 6	**Vittorio Garatti is born**.
1928	Jun. 14	Ernesto "Che" Guevara is born.
1936		Joaquín Weiss: *Arquitectura cubana colonial*
		Oscar Niemeyer, Lúcio Costa: Ministry of Education, Rio de Janeiro
1939		Eugenio Batista: Casa Falla Bonet, Havana
1940		Fulgencio Batista is elected president, with active support of PSP. He serves until 1944.
		New constitution outlaws racial segregation.
1943		ATEC: *Trinidad . . . lo que fue, es y será*, exhibition
1944		Eugenio Batista: Casa Batista, Havana
1945		Walter Gropius lectures in Havana.
1947		Luis Barragán: Casa Barragán, Tacubaya
		Colin Rowe: "Mathematics of the Ideal Villa"
		Francisco Prat Puig, *El prebarroco en Cuba—una escuela criolla de arquitectura morisca*
		"Quema de los Viñola," Frank Martínez, **Ricardo Porro**, Nicolás Quintana, Universidad de la Habana
1949		Frank Lloyd Wright: Laboratory Tower, Johnson Wax Co., Racine
		Philip Johnson: Johnson House, New Canaan
		Rudolf Wittkower: *Architectural Principles in the Age of Humanism*
		Silverio Bosch, Mario Romañach: Casa Noval, Havana
		Ricardo Porro graduates in architecture from the Universidad de la Habana.
		Ricardo Porro: Casa Armenteros, Havana
1950		**Ricardo Porro departs for postgraduate studies in Paris**.
1951		SOM (Gordon Bunshaft): Lever House, New York
		J. M. Coderich: ISM Apartment Block, Barcelona
		Eugenio Batista, Alberto Beale: *Los bateyes de los centrales azucareros*
		Harwell Hamilton Harris is appointed Director of the architecture school at the University of Texas. Bernard Hoesli, and Colin Rowe, followed by John Hejduk, Robert Slutzky et al. begin instituting innovative curriculum reforms.
		CIAM holds a series of classes in Venice taught by Ernesto Rogers, Giulio Carlo Argan, Le Corbusier, Carlo Scarpa, Bruno Zevi and others. **Ricardo Porro** attends.
1952		Alvar Aalto: Town Hall, Säynätsalo
		Le Corbusier: Unité d'Habitation, Marseille
		Alfonso Eduardo Reidy: Pedregulho housing, Rio de Janeiro
		Max Borges Jr.: Sala Arcos de Cristal, Club Tropicana, Havana
	Mar. 10	Fulgencio Batista seizes power in coup d'état and imposes seven-year dictatorship.
		Roberto Gottardi graduates Instituto Superiore di Architettura di Venezia.
		Founding of Arquitectos Unidos

		Ricardo Porro returns to Havana from Paris.
1953		Gabetti and d'Isola: Bottega d'Erasmo, Turin
		Harrison and Abramowitz: U.S. Embassy, Havana
		Oscar Niemeyer: Casa Niemeyer, Rio de Janeiro
		Silverio Bosch, Mario Romañach: Casa Aristigueta, Havana
		Ricardo Porro: Casa García, Havana
		Ricardo Porro, Nicolás Quintana, et al.: *Las villas pesqueras*
		Bruno Zevi: *La Poetica dell'architettura neoplàstica*
	March	Death of Joseph Stalin
	July	CIAM 9, Aix-en-Provence, Alison and Peter Smithson, Aldo van Eyck, Jacob Bakema and others form the nucleus of Team 10.
	July 26	Attack on Moncada Garrison in Santiago de Cuba. Fidel Castro and other survivors are imprisoned. "History will absolve me."
1954		Le Corbusier: Chapel of Nôtre-Dame-du-Haut, Ronchamp
		Mario Ridolfi: INA housing, Rome
		Bodiansky-Candilis-Woods: ATBAT housing, Algiers
		Aquiles Capablanca: Tribunal de Cuentas, Havana
		Ricardo Porro: Casa Villegas, Havana
		Max Bill et al., "Report on Brazil," *Architectural Review*
		Harwell Hamilton Harris: "Regionalism and Nationalism" (speech)
		Nikita Khrushchev, "Remove Shortcomings in Design, Improve work of Architects" (speech)
	Jan.	Team 10: *Doorn Manifesto*, "Statement on Habitat"
	June	CIA-sponsored coup overthrows democratically elected government of Guatemala. Che Guevara, as a visitor, witnesses the debacle.
	Nov.	Batista "elected" to second four-year term.
		Ricardo Porro travels to Mexico to meet Luis Barragán.
1955		Le Corbusier: Maison Sarabhai, Ahmedabad
		Josep Lluís Sert and Paul Lester Wiener consult on a master plan for Havana.
		Manuel Gutiérrez: Casa Verdera, Havana
		Moenck y Quintana: Cabañas, Hotel Kawama, Varadero
		Harwell Hamilton Harris resigns under pressure at the University of Texas. Hoesli, Rowe, Hejduk, Slutzky et al. are subsequently purged from the faculty
		Ernesto Rogers: "Le preesistenze ambientali e i termi practici contemporanei," *Casabella-Continuità*
		Henry-Russell Hitchcock, *Latin American Architecture Since 1945*, MoMA, New York
	Apr.	Amnesty granted by Batista for Moncada survivors in prison. Release and exile in Mexico where they found the July 26th Movement and begin guerrilla training.
		Founding of the Directorio Revolucionario led by architecture student José Antonio Echeverría
		Suppression of meetings of Arquitectos Unidos by Batista's BRAC
1956		Le Corbusier: Monastery of La Tourette
		Hans Scharoun, Girls' School, Lünen
		Eero Saarinen, Kresge Chapel, MIT
		Fruto Vivas: Club Táchira, Caracas
		Richard Neutra: Casa Schulthess, Havana
		Philip Johnson: Hotel and Casino Monaco (unbuilt project), Havana
		Moenck y Quintana: Casa Ramirez Corría
	Nov. 30	Uprising in Santiago organized by Frank País and Arturo Duque de Estrada
	Dec. 2	The Granma lands. Surviving rebels seek refuge in the Sierra Maestra.
1957		Luis Barragán (Mathias Goeritz): Towers for Ciudad Satélite, Mexico City

Mario Romañach: Casa Alvarez, Havana

Emilio del Junco: Casa del Junco, Havana

Ricardo Porro: Casa Ennis, Havana

Vittorio Garatti graduates from the Politécnico di Milano and departs for Venezuela.

Ricardo Porro: "El sentido de la tradición," *Noticias de Arte*

Death of Diego Rivera

First successful guerrilla campaigns in Sierra Maestra

Mar. 13   Failed attack on Presidential Palace led by Directorio Revolucionario. José Antonio
Echeverría, young architect and leader, is killed in a related action.

July 30   Assassination of Frank País in Santiago

Sept.   Navy uprising at Cienfuegos suppressed by government.

Nov.   **Roberto Gottardi departs for Venezuela**.

1958   Belgiojoso, Perressuti and Rogers (BBPR): Torre Velasca, Milan

Walter Gropius (TAC) and Pietro Belluschi: Pan American building, New York

Ludwig Mies van der Rohe: Seagram Building, New York

Fernando Salinas: Casa Higinio Miguel, Havana

Welton Beckett: Havana Hilton, Havana

April 9   The general strike fails.

Ricardo Porro departs for Venezuela.

Government offensive launched against guerrillas in Oriente.

August   Under commands of Che Guevara and Camilo Cienfuegos, the rebel army begins advance
across the island.

Dec. 28   Santa Clara falls, a decisive victory for Che Guevara.

Dec. 31   Fulgencio Batista leaves for Miami.

1959   Louis Kahn: Jewish Community Center Bathhouse, Trenton

Frank Lloyd Wright: Guggenheim Museum, New York

Paolo Soleri: Earth House, Scottsdale

Ralph Erskine, Kiruna Center, Norway

Otto Glaus: Airport, Lugano

Oscar Niemeyer: Chapel and Palace of the Dawn, Brasilia

Jan. 1   Victory declared by the Cuban Revolution.

Jan. 8   Fidel Castro arrives in Havana.

Feb. 1   Fidel Castro becomes Prime Minister; appoints Manuel Urrutia President.

March   Inaugural issue of *Lunes de la Revolución*, cultural review that spearheads an
explosion in the arts.

April   Reyner Banham publishes an attack on Ernesto Rogers, "Neoliberty—the Italian Retreat
from Modern Architecture," *Architectural Review*.

Seizure of casinos and imprisonment of Mafia boss Santo Trafficante Jr. in Havana

June   Ernesto Rogers counterattacks against Banham in "The Evolution of Architecture: Reply to
the Custodian of Frigidaires," *Casabella-Continuità*.

June   Walter Gropius agrees to write an article for *Integración* at the invitation of Hugo
Consuegra, Director of the Department of Fine Arts of the Ministry of Public Works.

May   First Agrarian Reform Law limits land holdings and initiates expropriations.

First Urban Reform Law limits the ownership of profit-producing property.

July 18   Manuel Urrutia, appointed President of Cuba, is constrained to resign in favor of Osvaldo
Dorticós.

Oct.   Aleksandr Alekseev and other senior KGB officers travel secretly to Havana to establish
contacts with members of revolutionary leadership.

Oct. 21   Huber Matos, commandante and military governor of Camagüey is accused of treason
and sentenced to twenty years in prison.

	Oct. 28	Airplane carrying Camilo Cienfuegos mysteriously disappears.
1960		Aldo van Eyck: Children's Home, Amsterdam
		Carlo Scarpa: Casa Beritti, Udine
		Jordi Bonet: Church of San Medi, Barcelona
		SOM (Natalie de Blois): Pepsi-Cola Co. headquarters, New York
		Candilis, Dony, Josic & Woods: Housing, Algiers
		Eladio Dieste: Church of Atlantide, Montevideo
		Carlos Raúl Villanueva: Ciudad Universitaria (begun in 1944), Caracas
	Jan.	Seizure by government of sugar plantations and large cattle ranches, many of which were U.S. owned
		Departure of Nicolás Quintana for Caracas and later Miami
	Feb. 13	Visit of Anastas Mikoyan, vice president of the USSR Counsel of Ministers and signing of first trade agreement
		Unidentified (CIA) planes fire bomb cane fields. Many other acts of sabotage ensue.
		Government closure of journals, *Diario de la Marina*, *Prensa Libre*, and *Carteles*
	March	Visit of Jean-Paul Sartre and Simone de Beauvoir
	June	Texaco, Esso and British Shell refineries are nationalized.
	July 3	Congress authorizes Eisenhower to cut sugar quota.
		Fidel Castro responds with a legal act that enables the nationalizing of U.S. property.
	July 23	First Trade Agreement with the Peoples' Republic of China
	Aug.	**Ricardo Porro returns to Cuba from Venezuela to work in urban planning**.
		Arrival of hitmen from Miami sponsored by the CIA and the Mafia to assassinate Cuban leaders.
		KGB changes code name for Cuba from *Yountsie* (Youngsters) to *Avanpost* (Bridgehead).
		More nationalizations of large US-owned business enterprises
	Sept.	Fidel Castro and Cuban delegation visits UN and stays at the Hotel Theresa in Harlem, receiving Khrushchev, Nasser, Nehru, Malcolm X, and others.
	Oct.	Sartre and de Beauvoir return to Cuba, pronounce revolutionary honeymoon over.
		Departure of Silverio Bosch for the US.
	Oct. 14	Second Urban Reform Law nationalizes all rental properties; owners can keep one home.
	Oct. 19	U.S. economic embargo, prohibits all exports except food and medicine.
	Oct. 25	166 more U.S. businesses and properties are nationalized.
	Dec.	**Vittorio Garatti and Roberto Gottardi arrive in Havana**.
1961		Le Corbusier: Carpenter Center, Harvard University
		Luis Barragán: Las Arboledas (begun 1957), Mexico City
		Walter Betancourt: Cultural Center, Velasco (completed 1991)
	Jan. 1	National Literacy Campaign begins.
		Fidel Castro calls for military mobilization and orders U.S. to cut embassy staff to 11.
	Jan. 3	U.S. breaks diplomatic relations with Cuba.
		Fidel Castro and Che Guevara play golf at the Country Club and decide to create an international school for the arts.
		Porro is given the "command" to begin designing the schools shortly thereafter. Within a short time he invites Garatti and Gottardi to join him.
	Feb.	CIA poisoned cigars caper launches a series of bizarre schemes to assassinate Cuban leaders.
		Departure of Humberto Alonso for Miami
	Apr. 16	After air attack on airports, Castro proclaims the Cuban Revolution socialist.
	Apr. 20	Victory over US-backed counterrevolutionaries at Playa Girón and Playa Larga in the bay of Pigs. John F. Kennedy accepts responsibility for the US-sponsored disaster.
		Design of the art schools escalates after the victory.

June		Castro's "Palabras a los intelectuales," define cultural principles: "within the Revolution everything; against the Revolution nothing."
		Sabá Cabrera Infante and Orlando Jiménez's film *PM* is banned. The cultural review *Lunes de Revolución* is suppressed.
		Castro praises the designs of Porro, Gottardi, and Garatti as "the most beautiful academy of arts in the world."
Aug.		Alliance for Progress is unveiled at the OAS summit in Punta del Este, Uruguay.
Sept.		**Construction on the art schools begins. Design continues as the three architects move their operations to the club house of the former country club.**
Oct.		Sino-Soviet split. Books by Mao are removed from Cuban bookstores.
Nov.		Kennedy authorizes $50 million for CIA Operation Mongoose to destabilize and overthrow Cuban government through espionage, sabotage, military attacks, and attempted assassinations.
		Crítica: cómo surgió la cultura nacional by Walterio Carbonell is banned and withdrawn from circulation three months after publication.
		First official persecution of gay Cubans who are rounded up and sent to reeducation camps
Dec. 2		Fidel Castro declares himself Marxist-Leninist.
Dec. 22		National Literacy Campaign officially ends.
1962		Eero Saarinen: Samuel F. B. Morse and Ezra Stiles College, Yale University
		Félix Candela: Chapel, Cuernavaca
		Jane Jacobs: *The Death and Life of Great American Cities*
		Khrushchev denounces modern art as deviant.
		Upon retirement from the school of architecture, Joaquín Weiss criticizes the growing bureaucratization and technocratization of architecture in Cuba, during his final lecture.
Jan.		OAS suspends membership for Cuba.
Feb. 3		Kennedy bans all exports to Cuba in an embargo with subsequently increasing restrictions.
Mar.		Purge of old-line communists. Anibal Escalante is sent into exile in Moscow. Founding of the Partido Unificado de la Revolución Socialista (PURS).
May 30		Cuba accepts USSR offer of nuclear missiles.
Oct.		October (Missile) Crisis. U.S. naval blockade of island. USSR agrees to withdraw missiles from Cuba, provoking strained relations between the two countries.
Nov.		Wifredo Lam's art is accused of being counterrevolutionary. **Ricardo Porro** and Carlos Franqui organize an exhibit defending him as a Marxist and revolutionary artist.
1963		Hans Scharoun: Philharmonic Hall, Berlin
		Paul Rudolph: Arts and Architecture Building, Yale University
		Charles Moore: Moore House, Orinda, California
		MLTW: Sea Ranch Condominium I, Mendocino
		Ricardo Porro: Hotel competition, San Sebastián, Spain
		Accusations of "counterrevolutionary" content are aimed at art works by Hugo Consuegra, Guido Llinás, and Tomás Oliva
July 8		Further tightening of U.S. embargo
		Guido Llinás leaves Cuba for Paris.
Sept.		VIIth International Congress of UIA held in Havana.
Oct. 4		Second Agrarian Reform Law nationalizes more farm land.
Nov. 22		Assassination of John F. Kennedy
		Colegio de Arquitectos and private architectural practice are officially abolished.
		Ricardo Porro resigns from architecture faculty.
		First *Gran Panel* factory for industrialized building donated by USSR.
		Allen Ginsberg visits and is expelled from Cuba.

1964		Carlo Scarpa: Castelvecchio Museum, Verona (begun 1956)

1964 Carlo Scarpa: Castelvecchio Museum, Verona (begun 1956)
Giovanni Michelucci: Church of San Giovanni Battista, Florence
Bernard Rudofsky, *Architecture Without Architects*
Humberto Alonso: CUJAE, Havana. (construction completed by others)
CIA-sponsored attacks against Cuba increase, hijackings, sabotage, armed commando raids against shipping.
Military coup in Brazil

Mar. Edith García Buchaca is removed as a political and cultural figure and is placed under house arrest for the remainder of her life.

Aug. Gulf of Tonkin "incident" provides pretext for U.S. escalation of the War in Vietnam.

Sept. OAS further tightens sanctions against Cuba.

Oct. Khrushchev is removed as Premier of USSR.

Oct. 25 Fidel Castro, "Closing Speech to the First Congress of Cuban Builders," calls for standardization and industrialization in building.

Nov. Richard M. Nixon is elected President.

1965 Louis Kahn: Salk Institute, La Jolla
Also Rossi: Monument to the Partisans, Segrate
Freidrich Kiesler, Sanctuary of the Book, Jerusalem
Vittorio Garatti: Soil and Fertilizer Technical Institute André Voisin, Güines
Fruto Vivas comes to Cuba as a volunteer architect for four years.

Mar. Architecture faculty and students form brigade to perform voluntary agricultural work in Matanzas.
Upon returning to Havana, a purge and restructuring of the architecture faculty places it under the authority of MICONS.

Apr. 25 Che Guevara departs for the Congo.

Apr. 28 U.S. occupies Santo Domingo with 20,000 troops.

July 26 **The National Art Schools are officially opened. Work is officially suspended.**

Oct. 3 The Partido Comunista de Cuba (PCC) is formally inaugurated, replacing the PURS which had incorporated the former July 26 Movement, the Directorio Revolucionario, and the PSP.

Oct. Guillermo Cabrera Infante leaves Cuba for diplomatic exile in Europe.
Hugo Consuegra publicly defends the schools and their architects in *Arquitectura Cuba*.

1966 Jørn Utzon: Opera House, Sydney
Peter Cook and Archigram: Plug-in City
Gian Carlo di Carlo: Student Housing, Urbino

Feb. Kwame Nkrumah in Ghana is overthrown by a CIA-supported coup.

Nov. Che Guevara arrives in Bolivia to attempt to foment a popular guerilla war.

July **Ricardo Porro leaves with his wife and son for Paris and establishes an architectural practice.**
Hugo Consuegra resigns from the architecture faculty and leaves Cuba for Spain.

1967 Salvador de Alba Martín: Market at San Juan de los Lagos, Jalisco, Mexico
Mario Coyula Cowley and Emilio Escobar Loret de Mola: Martyrs Park, Havana
Vittorio Garatti, Sergio Baroni and Hugo D'Acosta: Cuba Pavilion, Expo '67 Montreal
Reeducation camps for gays are closed in Cuba after protest by intellectuals.
Joaquín Rallo, dies of a heart attack in Jagüey Grande.

Oct. 8 Che Guevara is killed in Bolivia.

1968 Kevin Roche and John Dinkeloo: Ford Foundation, New York

George Collins, "The Transfer of Thin Masonry Vaulting from Spain to America," *Journal of the Society of Architectural Historians.*

Jan.   Walterio Carbonell, Sara Gómez, Manuel Granados and other leading Afro-Cuban intellectuals are punished for raising issues about racial inequities in the so-called "Black Manifesto" incident.

Mar. 31   Tet Offensive, Vietnam

April   Assassination of Martin Luther King Jr.

June   Assassination of Robert F. Kennedy

Guillermo Cabrera Infante, in exile, is expelled from the writer's union, UNEAC.

1974   June   **Vittorio Garatti is arrested, imprisoned for twenty-one days and expelled from Cuba.**

1982   Wifredo Lam dies in Paris.

1986   **Plans by Roberto Gottardi to renovate the schools are commissioned and shelved.**

1988   **Vittorio Garatti returns to visit Cuba.**

1989   The Berlin Wall is dismantled.

The National Art Schools are included in an exhibit of Cuban architecture at the CUJAE.

1995   **The art schools, and other contemporary works of architecture, are denied status as national landmarks.**

Apr.   **Exhibit at UNAICC of photographs by Hazel Hankin of the National Art Schools**

1996   Mar.   **Ricardo Porro returns to Cuba to give a series of public lectures.**

Cuban officials fail to sign off on application to the World Monuments Watch for the National Art Schools.

1997   Jan.   **Porro returns to Cuba again, this time at the invitation of Selma Díaz, to conduct a three-week charrette for architecture students. Meets with officials in the Ministry of Tourism regarding a project for a hotel in Varadero.**

The National Art Schools are officially declared a "Protected Zone."

Ernesto Jiménez García, *La Escuela Nacional de Artes*. This report sponsored by CENCREM surveys and estimates costs to restore the schools.

June   **Garatti returns again to Cuba and is invited to lecture at the Colegio de Arquitectos.**

1998   Jan.   Pope John Paul II visits Cuba.

May   **Porro participates in a symposium in Havana on Cuban modern architecture.**

July   **Vittorio Garatti meets with colleagues in Cuba and vacations with his wife at Varadero.**

Issue 377 of *Arquitectura Cuba* is dedicated to the work of Ricardo Porro.

Issue 378 of *Arquitectura Cuba* is dedicated to the work of Roberto Gottardi.

1999   Mar.   ***Revolution of Forms: Cuba's Forgotten Art Schools* is published, with launch events in Los Angeles and New York.**

Oct.   **At the national congress of the Union of Cuban Writers and Artists in its annual meeting with the Council of State, the importance and plight of the National Art Schools is publicly brought to the attention of Fidel Castro. Subsequently, the Cuban government commits to the preservation and restoration of the schools.**

Dec.   **Ricardo Porro, Vittorio Garatti, and Roberto Gottardi meet in Havana with high-level government officials to plan the preservation and restoration of the schools.**

BIBLIOGRAPHY

This bibliography reflects all known sources with any information about the National Art Schools and/or their architects. Some articles retrieved from personal archives in Cuba lacked full bibliographic information and are presented here as completely as possible. Many other sources which do not directly refer to the schools were used in the preparation of this text and are cited in the end notes.

Adamov, Arthur. "Cuba y el arte," *Pueblo y Cultura* (20 February 1964): 39–41.

Anon. "A Cluster of Bubbles," *Architectural Forum* 124, no. 1 (January/February 1966): 80–85.

Anon. "Cuban baroque," *Architectural Design* 36 (November 1966): 530.

Anon. "Deux Écoles de Danse de Ricardo Porro," *L'Architecture d'Aujourd'hui* 229, (October 1983): 88–97.

Baroni, Sergio. "Report from Havana," *Zodiac 8, International Review of Architecture* Renato Minetto, ed. (1993): 160–183.

Barré, François, and Isabelle Cazés. *Ricardo Porro*, Paris: Institut Français d'Architecture, Pandora Editions, 1991.

Bayón, Damián, and Paolo Gasparini. *The Changing Shape of Latin American Architecture—Conversations with Ten Leading Architects*, trans. Galen D. Greaser, 2nd ed. Chichester: John Wiley & Sons, 1979.

Blanch, Gilberto. "La ENA de Cubanacán para toda Cuba," (Unknown publication), 1974.

Boyer, Charles-Arthur, "Ricardo Porro," *Dictionnaire de l'Architecture Moderne et Contemporaine*. Jean-Paul Midant, ed., 718. Paris: Éditions Hazan/Institut Français d'Architecture, 1996.

Bullrich, Francisco. *New Directions in Latin American Architecture*, New Directions in Architecture. New York: George Braziller, 1969.

Carley, Rachel. *Cuba, 400 Years of Architectural Heritage*. New York: Whitney Library of Design, 1997.

Carmona, Darío. "Dos Ciudades de la Imaginación—Escuelas de Arte de La Habana," *Cuba* 30 (3 October 1964): 34–53.

Collins, George. "The Transfer of Thin Masonry Vaulting from Spain to America," *Journal of the Society of Architectural Historians* 27, no. 3 (October 1968): 176–201.

Cortesi, Isota. "Vittorio Garatti: Scuole d'Arte a Cuba, Avana, (1961–1964)," *Area* 35 (November/December): 16–27.

Coyula Cowley, Mario. "Cuban Architecture its History and its Possibilities," *Cuba Revolution and Culture* 2 (1965): 12–25.

Castro Ruz, Fidel. "Palabras a los intelectuales," 30 June 1961, quoted in *Noticias de Hoy* (4 May 1963).

Consuegra, Hugo. "Las Escuelas Nacionales de Arte," *Arquitectura Cuba* 334 (1965): 14–21.

———. unpublished memoirs, 1996 and 1998.

Cruz, Soledad. "Reflejar la vida del pueblo: XIII aniversario de la ENA," (Unknown publication), 18 February, 1975.

Dorfles, Gillo. *Architetture Ambigue, Dal Neobarocco al Postmoderno*, vol. 8, Immagine e Consumo. Bari: Edizioni Dedalo, 1984.

Dumont, Marie-Jeanne. "Porro rue Paul Eluard á Saint-Denis," *Architecture d'Aujourd'hui* 270 (September 1990): 82–85.

Duverger, Heriberto. "Mis Años Felices," unpublished article: 1992.

Fernández, Urbano & Eliseo Diego. "El arte de una escuela," *Cuba Internacional* (May 1975): 31–38.

Ferrari, Alberto. "Cuba," *Casabella* 354 (January 1970): 9–16.

Fiorese, Giorgio. *Architettura e istruzione a Cuba*. Milan: CLUP, 1980.

———. "Due architetture di Vittorio Garatti a 9000 chilometri e 15 anni de destanza," *Modo* 6 (April 1982): 38–48.

Gaillard, Marc. "Barroquismo y sensualidad/Nuevo Estilo Cubano de Arquitectura," *Pueblo y Cultura* (24 June 1964): 12–15.

Garatti, Vittorio. "Ricordi di Cubanacán," *Modo* 6 (April 1982): 47–48.

Goldberger, Paul. "Annals of Preservation, Bringing Back Havana," *The New Yorker* (26 January 1998): 50–61.

Goulet, Patrice. *Ricardo Porro*, 2 vols., Partitions, Paris: Institut Français d'Architecture, 1993.

———. "Defense et illustration du romantisme: Trois soirées avec Ricardo Porro," *Architecture d'Aujourd'hui* 224 (December 1982): 64.

Gutiérrez, Ramón. *Arquitectura y Urbanismo en Iberoamérica*. Madrid: Manuales Arte Catedra, 1992.

Hankin, Hazel, *Hazel Hankin Fotografias—Abril 1995*. With essays by Eliana Cardenas and Jesús Vega, Havana: Colegio de Arquitectos UNAICC, 1995.

Jiménez García, Ernesto. *La Escuela Nacional de Artes (Información General)*, Havana: CENCREM, 1997.

Liernur, Jorge Francisco. "Un nuevo mundo para el espiritu nuevo: los descubrimientos de América Latina por la cultura arquitectonica del siglo XX," *Zodiac 8, International Review of Architecture*, Renato Minetto, ed. (1993): 85–121.

Loomis, John A. "Revolutionary Design," *Loeb Fellowship Forum* 2, no. 1 (Summer 1995): 4–5.

———. "Architecture or Revolution?—The Cuban Experiment," *Design Book Review*, John A. Loomis, ed. (Summer 1994): 71–80.

López Oliva, Manuel. "Trece años de enseñanza artistica," (Unknown publication), 3 January 1975.

López Rangel, Rafael. *Arquitectura y Subdesarrollo en America Latina*. Puebla: Universidad Autónoma de Puebla, 1975.

Martin Zequeira, Maria Elena. "Arquitectura: hallar el marco poético," interview with Ricardo Porro, *Revolución y Cultura* 5 (1996): 44–51.

Nakamura, Toshio. "Ricardo Porro," *A+U* 282, (March 1994): 4–93.

Noever, Peter, ed. *The Havana Project—Architecture Again*. Munich: Prestel Verlag, 1996.

Porro, Ricardo. "El sentido de la tradición," *Nuestro Tiempo* 16, año IV (1957).

———. "El Espacio en la Arquitectura Tradicional Cubana," *Arquitectura Cuba* 332: 27–36.

———. "Wifredo Lam," (Unknown publication, 1962): 46–48.

———. "Ricardo Porro—Écoles d'Art à la Havane," *L'Architecture d'Aujourd'hui* 119, (March 1965): 52–56.

———. "La Casa es una obra de arte," (Unknown publication).

———. "Cinq Aspects du Contenu en Architecture," *PSICON—Rivista Internazionale de Architettura* 2/3 (January/June 1975): 153–69.

———. "Couleur et architecture, une longue histoire," *Architecture Intérieure CREE* 171 (May 1979): 64–68.

———. "Cuba y Yo," *Escandalar—Cuba Otra* 17–18 (January/June 1982): 152–156.

Portoghesi, Paolo. *Postmodern*. New York: Rizzoli International, 1983.

———. "Gespräch mit Ricardo Porro," *UMRISS* 3+4, (1985): 89–112.

———. *Dopo l'architettura moderna*. Moderna: Biblioteca di Cultura, 1989.

———. "Une architecture romantique," *La Havane 1952–1961*, Série Mémoires 31, Éditions Autrement, (May 1994): 39–41.

Quintana, Nicolás. "Evolución Histórica de la Arquitectura en Cuba—Epoca Republicana (1900–1959)," *La Enciclopedia de Cuba*. San Juan: Enciclopedia y Clasicos Cubanos, 1977.

Ragon, Michel. *Histoire Mondiale de l'Architecture et de l'Urbanisme Moderne*. vol. 2 of 2 vols, Paris: Casterman, 1972.

Reyes Ceballos, Mariano. "Escuela Nacional de Arte: 25 años después," *Juventud Rebelde* (4 December 1987).

Rodríguez, Eduardo Luis. "La década incógnita, Los cincuenta: modernidad, identidad y algo más," *Arquitectura Cuba* 376 (1997): 36–43.

———. *La Habana—Arquitectura del Siglo XX*. Leopoldo Blume, ed., with introduction by Andrés Duany. Barcelona: Editorial Blume, 1998.

Rainer, Roland. "Architektur in Kuba Leute, Architektur und Kunst in Wien," *UMRISS* (March/April, 1985).

Rowntree, Diana. "The New Architecture of Castro's Cuba," *Architectural Forum* (April 4, 1964): 122–125.

Ryan, Raymund. "Outrage," *Architectural Review* (June 1996): 21.

Seguí Diviñó, Gilberto, "En defensa de la arquitectura," *El Caimán Barbudo* 22, no. 254 (January 1989): 12–13, 18.

———. "Les odeurs de la rue," *La Havane 1952–1961*, Série Mémoires 31, Éditions Autrement, (May 1994): 27–38.

Segre, Roberto, *La Arquitectura de la Revolución Cubana*. Montevideo: Facultad de Arquitectura Universidad de la Republica, 1968.

———. *Diez Años de Arquitectura Revolucionaria en Cuba*. Cuadernos de la Revista Unión, Havana: Ediciones Union, 1969.

———. *Cuba—Arquitectura de la Revolución*. Colección Arquitectura y Crítica, Barcelona: Editorial Gustavo Gili, 1969.

———. *Cuba—l'Architettura della Rivoluzione.* Quaderni di Architettura e Urbanistica 18, Venice: Marsilio Editori, 1977.

———. "Continuitá e rinnovamento nell'architettura cubana del XX secolo," *Casabella* 446, (February 1981): 10–19.

———. *Arquitectura y Urbanismo de la Revolución Cubana.* Havana: Editorial Pueblo y Educación, 1989.

_____. *Lectura Crítica del Entorno Cubano.* Havana: Editorial Letras Cubanas, 1990.

———. *America Latina Fim de Milénio.* São Paolo: Studio Nobel, 1991.

———. "Tres décadas de arquitectura cubana: La herencia histórica y el mito de lo nuevo," *Arquitectura Antillana del siglo XX.* Universidad Autónoma Metropolitana-Unidad Xochimilco: Mexico City, 1993.

———. "La Habana siglo XX: espacio dilatado y tiempo contraído," *Ciudad y Territorio, Estudios Territoriales* XXVIII (110), 1996.

Segre, Roberto and Rafael López Rangel, *Architettura e territorio nell'America Latina. Saggi & Documenti,* trans. Savino D'Amico. Milan: Electa Editrice, 1982.

Torre, Susana. "Architecture and Revolution: Cuba, 1959 to 1974," *Progressive Architecture* (October 1974): 84–91.

Vásquez, Omar. "Celebran jornada por XX aniversario de la Escuela Nacional de Arte," (Unknown publication), 12 December 1981.

———. "More than ideas and dreams: already realities of the Revolution: Culture in the Revolution—Achievements in art education," *Granma* (17 June 1979): 7.